T0196393

MENTAL ILLNESS MI
Doesn't Look Like ME

A Warrior's Intimate Struggle to Confront
Mental Health Illness Face-to-Face

Susie L. Landown-Clarke CPT, ret., MBA

authorHOUSE®

AuthorHouse™
1663 Liberty Drive
Bloomington, IN 47403
www.authorhouse.com
Phone: 1 (800) 839-8640

Published by AuthorHouse 06/29/2017

ISBN: 978-1-5462-0205-9 (sc)
ISBN: 978-1-5462-0206-6 (hc)
ISBN: 978-1-5462-0204-2 (e)

Library of Congress Control Number: 2017911752

Print information available on the last page.

Contents

A Foreword of Truths

Mental illness is an epidemic without boundaries that I reflect on in both my spiritual and occupational calling. My sister suffered combat-induced distress that produced psychological overload, with an inability to functionally cope. The difficulty is recognizing the devastation and havoc caused by this health infirmity, which expands its scope from adolescence to adulthood. Daily, I witness fear-filled eyes of mental-illness sufferers who are in search of answers but overwhelmingly troubled and unable to express or accept their own truths. The darkness that overshadows mental illness sometimes prevents affirmation about the invasion of the disease.

Although mental illness is full of complexities, its most awkward complication may be societal stigmas. I believe that misconstrued stigmas endanger continual treatment and therapy, which is vital to recovery. Consequently, stigmas surrounding mental illness can sometimes become enablers that deny or defer treatment—all because of human misconceptions.

Society must recognize that increasing awareness and support programs are necessary to promote mental healthiness. However, there is yet a more powerful serenity of healing to free the mind from darkness. Shunning of mental illness is a reality for many sufferers, causing isolation, seclusion, and loneliness. Mockery of any illness is intolerable, especially to the degree that it prevents people from seeking critical support services.

Thousands if not millions suffer from mental illness and are, as a result, at risk of suicide, homicide, and additional societal detriments.

Stigmas that ostracize ill patients may encourage sufferers to keep the illness private, even though recuperation requires public resources. Isolation is one of the most harmful detriments to not only the ill person but also the ill-informed public. The truth is what we all discern: "The mind is a terrible thing to waste." Moreover, "The mind is already a waste if it is dysfunctional!"

The author was a pillar of strength for her family and a professional trailblazer throughout her military career. She gave nearly twenty-two years of service, but near the end of her career, something unknown surfaced that devastated her quality of life. It was years after returning from the war that she began to unravel, becoming mentally and emotionally dysfunctional. My sister's mind seemed to faint without sense, causing an intensification that induced depressive moods and panic with anxieties. This was awkward, because none of us dared to address these behavioral abnormalities as an issue, assuming it was due to life stressors along with the demands of family and career.

As a sibling, I was surprised to learn about these detriments, because of my sister's strength and resiliency to endure no matter the challenge. She has always been outspoken, outgoing, and outstandingly fruitful, but this was no longer the case. It became evident that something unusual was taking hold the minute my sister began isolating herself from others, especially those she loved. This book demonstrates exactly why mental illness is a growing epidemic. If it does not look like the image we hold, we do not recognize it. It is like a hidden image that escapes our perception, disguised by contrasting contexts. It is curiously invisible to insight because it clandestinely secretes itself.

This book is filled with information about the subversive power of mental illness, which inadvertently induces psychological havoc, including suicide. The author shares deranging, psychosomatic episodes experienced as a combat veteran who refused to become consumed by mental illness. This was a ghastly yet unexpected medical diagnosis that required intense therapy, treatment, and medication. After years of battling mental illness's painful turmoil, the author realized that her road to recovery required something more potently compelling, which was a divine healing.

We discover the author's silent fears from the onset of the story. She clearly and often suggests that mental illness is one of the most stigmatized diseases that is purposefully veiled, camouflaging distresses and societal perceptions. I personally witnessed this imminent mental crisis on several occasions. My beloved sister unleashed fiery rage, raw emotions, and resentment that compounded the severity of undiagnosed symptoms.

Throughout this intimate account of mental illness, my sister seemed skeptical about her diagnosis. I suppose denial was the most obstructive barrier that possibly delayed her treatment. Mental illness led her to even question her identity relevant to family and career. Her lack of self-relevance almost resulted in her demise. The author regained a sense of relevance through recovery instead of surrendering to emotional remorse.

Mental illness apparently ascends when there are mounting psychological imbalances, causing the mind to become yoked to trauma. The writer's desire was to acknowledge the prevalence of the illness but not to own the illness, mitigating persistent psychological suffering and discord. I am confident that many sufferers would not share such intimate details so nakedly about their mental illness without spiritual fruition and healing.

This story is a testimony to conquering external fears that suffocate internal feelings, realizing the heavenward power above all. I applaud this author. This is a courageous story that can inspire desolate minds while provoking deductive thinking. Suffering is inevitable in many cases. However, when the mind suffers, the body oftentimes descends into unhealthy alignments of synchronism with little to no desire to resist the ravages of distress and discomposure. Therefore, we must address the suffering of the mind to impede psychological afflictions, so that hope is tangible for those dealing with mental illness.

Dr. Tyrona Landown
DCC/Evangelist

Acknowledgments

Thank you to my darling husband, James Clarke Jr., for embracing me throughout this journey of redemption. Your love, patience, and caring hands held me close, interlinking our heartbeats. I never knew which beat was mine or yours—all because the beat synchronized our souls.

Parriz, Jostein, and Landowyn, you are my everything. Living and not having any of you would leave me lifeless. I thank God for blessing me with distinct beings at different times, all unique in their own skins.

My most cherished roles: wife and mother.

Preface

Summoned by a Stranger

This book is based my experience and insight, aiming to provide an intimate account of struggling, battling, and defeating mental illness. This is a rare opportunity for the public to witness this illness in its rawest context from a firsthand account that describes the emotional and psychological suffering inflicted by mental illness. I will share the defenseless vulnerabilities of losing one's mind and health, and my fear of being tucked away in seclusion by a confining force that seemed demonic.

Mental illness is like a thief that is too clever to surrender even when caught red-handed. It still expects to carry out its malicious intent—to steal, destroy, and kill if necessary. Mental illness was the thief aiming to rob me of my health. My struggles are penned in this epic journey of recovery as I battled a heartless foe while undergoing alternating temperaments of highs and lows. I was diagnosed with PTSD, severe depression, acute anxiety, memory loss, debilitating migraines, panic disorders, and bipolar disorder.

We all know our name, and perhaps we remember other details about our lives. However, when something traumatic like an illness occurs, we begin to contemplate so many other questions, because many things that once were certain now appear uncertain. Of course I knew my name, but the alarming thing was that I did not know exactly who or what my essence was, to myself or anyone else.

I began to confront my own being by asking questions like: Who am I? What is my context? What are my traits? Why am I different? All these basic questions may seem simplistic, but suddenly something changed, and I did not know what it was.

We are humans, but I did not feel human. I was rooted in an absolute reality at times and non-absolute idealism in others, as if I was imagining things in a faraway land. I saw myself; I could touch myself; I heard when I spoke; I could smell scents. The one thing that had vanished from my sense of being was my ability to feel emotions.

Deep within this new world that was unimaginably far away, nothing was absolute anymore. I was alive, but was I really living? Life became an art of transformational change, painting me into complete chaos where mental illness offered only shaded grays.

At some point, I started to accept that I had become colorless. Ironically, not only had my mental capacities vanished, but now even my physical self was fading like a ghostly shadow, occupying all filled and vacant space surrounding my bodily width. The things that I am expressing seem more like a fantasy or a movie script, but in all truth these facades of my existence had become factual. It may be difficult to surmise that my reality had become a secluded illusion, but it was merely an authorized venue to escape to so I could avoid facing the detriments of mental illness.

My life appeared to change far too often from calm to chaos, and I could no longer differentiate between the two. Once this mental illness entered my sacred circle of life, it was obvious that I had become unsound. I am alluding to the evolution of my disappearance, even though my appearance was evident. I had lost the ability to express simple things or do simple tasks that were once as easy as reciting the alphabet.

Even my responses when communicating in simple dialect drew stares or were viewed as improper in nature, which often rattled my family. I was a raging bull to those who loved me the most. I suppose once this explicit and sometimes implicit change occurred, my emotional behavior, my mental capacity, and my inability to cope influenced the dominance of mental illness. These profound instabilities ultimately kept me from seeking proper therapies.

My journey revealed that therapy is different from one person to another. However, there are some humane therapies that, collectively activated, were healing for me: love, acknowledgment, support, and time (LAST). These allowed me to grasp that my recovery could endure and not perish to the will of my mental illness and disorders.

Society has for years muted millions of vulnerable cries of those suffering from mental illness. Many sufferers' and advocates' voices have been muffled. This muting may have inadvertently contributed to the seclusion and silence of mental illness sufferers because they felt shunned by society. I strongly believe it is an egregious act to ignore suffering from any type of illness, especially when it impacts an individual's mental functioning. In my view, mental illness has the capacity to create depletion of thought and memory, which puts the sufferer and society at volatile risk.

Previously, I viewed mental illness as an unconcerned bystander, lacking empathy or compassion while focusing on other priorities. Little did I know that I was about to be chosen. It was mysterious even to me that I would become the outcast in an unfamiliar world that I had previously ignored. It was no longer a joke; it had become my reality. I was summoned by an illness that began to cause havoc in my mind, body, and soul. This was not a request; it was more like a command to comply.

It was like the American judicial system in which citizens are summoned to serve as jurors, and they often make every effort to be excused from a duty of obligation. Nonetheless, it is rare that one is excused, whether against one's will or due to other obligations. I was caught in this exact situation. There was nothing or no one able to excuse my attendance, no matter how hard I tried to resist or be excluded. I became the prey among a world of aloof people.

Although this journey is insightful, it is also extremely painful. Nonetheless, sharing my encounters with mental illness is the only way to offer sensitivity and insight while expanding awareness. I am inviting you to experience the silence and shame of being present but absent. This is not a place of laughter or joy but a raw account that offers an outsider the opportunity to grasp the depths of mental illness as a guest of one who is affected.

Not everyone understands or has witnessed mental illness up close and personal, which I believe allows human perceptions to vary in such a wide range of realities. The invite is not to celebrate with gossipy conversations but to galvanize compassion for those who suffer from mental illness—to foster a sense of harmony rather than havoc. I believe when people feel included, they become more engaged. Suddenly, unexpected responses can emerge, presenting the most precious gift imaginable: a listening ear with a caring heart.

I am offering a one-of-a-kind invitation to partake in this social conversation. We must mobilize efforts so that we can be enlightened about the unfamiliarity and difficulty faced by one who encounters the ever-changing motives of mental illness. I experienced motionless movements and moods. My emotions would some days start off like a slow dance and then speed up unexpectedly to a ballet routine, evolving into disco, then pop, and suddenly a hop and a skip. It takes skill to dance to a tune that is abrupt and offers no warning. Likewise, mental illness is a dance that is off beat one minute and then seconds later on again, causing extreme missteps.

The book's title substantiates the perceptiveness of many who are unaware of mental illness. I often hear people ask about what mental illness is or isn't, which is a telltale sign that mental illness is faceless to so many. The title *Mental Illness: MI Doesn't Look Like ME* is not about race, gender, socioeconomic status, or any worldly things. It's far deeper, because when I gaze in the mirror, my vision is not what I visualize; it is what I breathed and struggled with daily for over five years. I struggled to communicate, associate with, and interact with others.

Mental illness must no longer be portrayed as what we think it traditionally looks like, because that proves irrational. Thinking that way has for far too long been an implanted perception. Many of us may assume it's a person acting in a visibly erratic way—foaming at the mouth, nodding back and forth in a chair, or tucked away in some mental institution. I beg to differ, because neither of these images is true to my experience. Now, as I come out of this dark, secluded closet, I envision ways that society has been bamboozled for decades if not centuries.

Mental illness stigmas still exist because society is afraid to even acknowledge it as a disease caused by traumatic events or experiences. Perhaps most of those suffering from mental illness are functioning at some capacity to turn away from the joy of living as a survival pretense. Contrary to such belief, I looked somewhat normal externally in the presence of others, leading them to assume my normalcy. However, internally, I was dysfunctional in so many ways.

I think the only improvement in Western civilization has been the acknowledgement of mental illness's existence, simply because of the publicized behavioral actions of those suffering and speaking as candid, reflective voices. The transparent behavior surrounding mental suffering thus far has likely proved a public misconception. I realized that the norm is now abnormal in detecting who is or isn't suffering from mental illness. It is not as detectable as one may think, especially for those who do not appear physically ill or fitful. This is possibly the most deceptive allegation of all, since most sufferers aim to entomb their symptomatic behaviors.

I suspect that mental illness is so unpredictable for some sufferers because if most are candid, there persists a struggle to maintain self-control. This does not suggest that each of us is a ticking time bomb, but it explains why rage can occur so suddenly, as we have a varying range of responsiveness. Loss of self-control can result in an outburst, vile language, or physical acting out, as well a silent response that illustrates disdain for something or someone. I oftentimes displayed emotions like these to convey my feelings without having to share my thoughts. On occasion, complex emotions erupted without warning, causing an overload of anxiety as I feared exclusion and rejection.

I can recall instances where I was conversing with people in a calm, appropriate manner and suddenly something that person said triggered my emotions and things spun out of control. I would yell, scream, and shout profanities. The evil that lurked in my eyes surely made others feel uncomfortable or fearful, especially loved ones.

I recall one of my children responding in a manner that I did not anticipate during a moment of scolding. It was apparent that communicative behaviors were not as they should be between parent and child during this emotional encounter. Nonetheless, I viewed the child's response as combative and oppressive, as if my opinion did not matter. I responded by picking up an object and striking the child in the head. At this point, I had not been diagnosed, but I recognized something was unfamiliar.

My response was insensitive, as was my reaction in responding to my injured child. Seconds later, after realizing what I had done, I bandaged the child's injury, but I felt no remorse. I was emotionally frozen, without any regard for my actions. Episodes like this led me to distance myself from both outsiders and insiders, shredding my support system to threads because of the spiraling effects of mental illness.

I no longer feel rejected, shameful, or imprisoned by the multilayered mental illnesses that interrupted my life. Mental illness was emotionally infectious, causing pain and afflictions that hindered me from health prosperity for five years. My mental illness diagnoses included severe depression, multilayered anxieties, PTSD, and memory loss, which contributed to other disorders.

I am now a voice advocating for myself and other sufferers as to why mental illness is an encaging phobia. I was not physically encaged, but mentally I felt locked away in seclusion that necessitated silence. There were no physical bars to barricade my body; the walls of fear were invisible, as if a sensor kept me confined. I became silent without realizing my seclusion was self-inflicted. It was merely to keep me from being ridiculed by strangers.

Frankly, it was necessary to seclude myself from even family and friends at times because I felt detached from my role as a mom, wife, sibling, and friend. Mental illness is coated with anxieties and fears for those of us suffering, as well those who surround us. Please do not shun us any further by ignoring our pleas for help. Please stop viewing those with mental illness as unstable weaklings who should be ignored. Denying valid concerns surrounding mental illness is shameful, because it is undeniably a growing epidemic in both adults and adolescents. Ignoring the risks can lead to further silence, ostracism, and misdiagnosis, which can in turn result in danger to the public. Instead, I ask for advocacy for increased treatment, therapies, and most critically, helping hands from strangers without pre-rooted judgments.

> *Therefore, let us stop passing judgment on one another. Instead, make up your mind not to put any stumbling block or obstacle in the way of a brother or sister.*
>
> *— Romans 14:13*

My personal experience confirms that most people with mental illness need no additional obstacles or barriers in their lives. For decades, many sufferers have been barricaded by fears that are puzzling even to ourselves. I felt locked away and disowned by those I trusted the most. It is hard to imagine being judged when an illness consumes you, yet that's when people see fit to injure you the most.

Funny thing is that there was no more space internally or externally for superficial wounds. My body was buried with invisible distresses. This illness does not look like me because society has deemed it to be ghostly, allowing us to be further incapacitated— subdued in a mental state but also an emotional state that produces cerebral inactivity.

I have suffered from an array of mental illnesses that were triggered by contributing variables. These variables were possibly symptomatic from childhood and certainly adulthood. For instance, some of the trauma arose from multiple head injuries, career stress, childbirth, combat, and possibly being a child of man who suffered from mental illness after returning from the Vietnam War. Prior to an unexpected diagnosis, I was a smart, accomplished, thriving, and successful career woman. I was a college graduate, military officer, healthy middle-aged soldier, wife, and mom. It seemed as though I had it all—or at least the appearance of it, as that was all there was to be seen from an exterior viewpoint.

Mental illness is a part of me. It may never allow me to return to my old self, but who wants to be the same old person as yesterday or even a year past? I am not glad to have experienced different encounters with mental illnesses or disorders, but I am oh so grateful to be able to share some of the dark accounts, the struggles, and my road to recovery. I now breathe relief and not regret, because not every sufferer will recover from mental illness, which is the most disheartening confession for such a suppressing battle.

At one time, the idea of being ridiculed for incompetency was just as remote as the location in which I battled threats by foreign enemies. To me, as to many others, having any symptoms or signs of an ailment was not seen as warrior-like. My goal was to acknowledge my illness, not to own it, for I emphatically trust that the new me is so much more content with what I have evolved into.

Just imagine standing next to me at an event where people are chatting and socializing without a care in the world. Suddenly, I approach and introduce myself. What would be your response, even though I am a stranger? Most likely, you would offer some type of greeting and share your name, with perhaps some small talk about the event. Unless I acted abnormally or in some unusual manner, your presumption of me would be that I seem balanced. Mental illness hides beneath layered surfaces and is often hard to detect, so most times the sufferer is made to feel or appear normal, suggesting that things are all right when in fact they are all wrong.

Don't be twisted in your thinking or engagement with people like me who have in the past or are currently suffering from mental illness by our outward appearances. It is the inner ambience of emotions that is the most moving at any present time. If someone appears intact, it can truly be a disguise, much different from what you will see when you become more attuned to his or her actions.

In some instances, depending upon the mental illness, an aware individual may be able to detect that something is peculiar. Mental illness is more common than you may think among the groups of people who surround you, whether at work, home, or leisure.

Many people are in the presence of friends, family, and coworkers every day, yet they seem flabbergasted once something behavioral happens. Oftentimes, the echoed statement is that the individual appeared normal and no one noticed anything unusual. I find that difficult to accept, because there is always someone who noticed something. That person chose to either ignore it or to disbelieve what they were witnessing.

I caution you to not become complacent as to the stability of those in your circle but remember to think outside of the box when noticing eyebrow-raising behaviors of friends or loved ones. I believe these are a cry for help, but the cry may appear in soundless forms like seclusion, detachment, rage, antisocial behavior, communication barriers, anxiousness, panic, and many more. These are some of the behavioral signs I showed, which caused me to fear someone finding out.

From a mental illness perspective, it was painful for me to be walled or confined with no way to convey what was happening. I felt forbidden by society's phobic stigmas to share this extreme darkness because of the impact to my career, people's perception of me, and my own self-image. I was victimized by a systemic culture that I sincerely believed would have penalized me severely through demotion or ostracism.

When I became detained by mental illness, the strongholds of the disease became more empowered to victimize my will to fight. After five long years of dealing with this intense health confrontation, I am ready to share private encounters in an audible, public forum with strangers. I will reveal to you the depths of my psychological and emotional strangeness.

Usually, if one is asked or invited to an event, there is the subtle expectation to present the host with something more than just your presence; this, my beloved, is no different. The difference is that the most desired gift from you to me as an ex-mental illness sufferer is to be cerebrally cognizant. It is essential that we have a spirited consciousness to spearhead awareness of this illness as a public crisis, although it is often perceived as a private cause. It is a public crisis because those ailing from mental illnesses are physically rooted throughout communities that often negate the social detriments surrounding the illness. Nevertheless, it is a private matter because the sufferer is individually yet inadvertently entangled in a web of emotional despair that is distressing to share openly.

This crisis yearns for communal investments to cultivate individual alertness as well as collective awareness. Research data from the National Alliance on Mental Illness (NAMI) suggests that mental illness and mental health disorders are on an upswing, becoming more prevalent during adolescent years, although often going undetected or untreated. It is important that society examines the contributing factors surrounding these rising rates.

It would be mindless of me to not engage the significance of your attendance. Please be on your best behavior as you learn about the vulnerabilities and fears of someone who suffered from mental illness. It is not a joke. I am not desiring sympathy, but most definitely, at a minimum, empathy. In this instance, my gratitude is for efforts to become more perceptive in encounters with those struggling with mental illness. Keep these statistics in mind:

- 20 percent of youth ages thirteen to eighteen live with a mental health condition.
- 11 percent of youth have a mood disorder.
- 10 percent of youth have a behavior or conduct disorder.
- 8 percent of youth have an anxiety disorder.
- 1 in 5 adults in America experience a mental illness.
- Nearly 1 in 25 (10 million) adults in America live with a serious mental illness.
- Half of all chronic mental illness begins by the age of fourteen, and three quarters by the age of twenty-four.

The information above can be found at www.nami.org.

My desire to research and learn more about mental health illness was intense as well overwhelming at times because of the need to examine multiple resources. My painful journey reveals the pitfalls of mental illnesses, the complexities of multilayered disorders, and my road to recovery. I am eager to share my story with millions as a way to inspire optimism.

I hope you are encouraged, enlightened, and engaged to facilitate breaking down walls that isolate anyone suffering from mental illness. I believe subdued silence is possibly the most alarming threat imaginable. Invisible walls unsympathetically enslaved my mind as I suffered from mental illness. This book is based upon my own insight, which includes personal, intimate experiences. As I struggled with the demise of my health, professional diagnosis revealed transformational variances, including chronic PTSD, severe depression, extreme anxiety, memory loss, debilitating migraines, panicking fears, and claustrophobia.

The summation of my illness encounters has inspired me to address unreasonable accounts of mediocre health care for veterans. My intention is no longer to question the availability of mental health aid but perhaps to become an active voice in broadcasting awareness. Improved programs and resources will undeniably help prevent further ravaging of our heroic women and men who served so valiantly with honor.

Chapter 1

Stranger ... Who, Me?

E ven though I know my name, I feel and appear anonymous. I have lost familiarity with who I am or imagine myself to be. Many unknown yet new discoveries are upon me, and I am afraid to take the next step. However, as I walk in dismay, I notice that although the sun is vibrantly shining, darkness still creeps in.

My shadowy silhouette seems to step before me, instead of me before my shadow, causing me to become second in command of my own life. The involuntary relinquishing of my self-power was the unveiling of the mystery that led to my transfiguration into a stranger. My mystifying belief is that I need a new introduction to both myself and the society that embodies my core.

I am not exactly sure how to convey such a simplistic query as the metamorphosis of my intellect, but there are some things I do believe. If I had been allowed to be open about my struggles with mental illness, my self-acquaintance may have never permitted me to become self-alienated. People within society hoard so many opinions, misconceptions, and biases about other people that I preferred to avoid dealing with another blatantly discriminative stigma about my mental illness. The uncertainties and fears that I struggled with contributed to my voluntary secrecy, coaxing me to encage myself and my emotions as I sidelined myself in this game of substituted life.

I am not only unknown to you but as well, oftentimes, I am foreign to myself. We are strangers amongst strangers until that first verbal encounter, handshake, or visual connection that sparks dialogue. Oddly, I wonder about interactive connections of empathy for those we know and those we do not know. For instance, there were people I interacted with daily who were completely clueless about the painful disorders I was suffering. Conversely, we cheer as fans for sports teams of people we don't know, never met, or perhaps only relate to as avid sport fanatics. I wonder, why is it so difficult for a humane society to render sensitivity in cheering for wellness in the aspect of defeating an opponent? Certainly, more than anything else, the most important game of all is the game of life.

Mental illness is like a competitive sport, where haters are trying to detract you from being a conscious winner. It has been said that mental strength is the will to win more so than physical strength or capability. There were times when I competed every day and every minute with this foe of mental illness. I tried to rise above it, believing it was not by predilection but perhaps probability. This opposition of force attacked as I stood defenseless and exposed, with no strategy to defeat this suffocating, offensive opponent. I was always on defense because the ball was never in my court. Imagine having to play defense for an entire game! It was exhausting. I feared I would not win but lose against this raging foe, this relentless opponent.

Mental illness was like an out-of-body experience, akin to a supernatural possession. Some unknown demonic power had dug its gripping fingers deep within, piercing my soul. Ultimately, this evil power instigated an invasive level of persuasion that spewed ghostly gestures and antagonized me to surrender and give up. My urge or desire to be mentally and emotionally free were clearly under attack. It appeared I had lost the game of life to an opponent I knew nothing about, nor did I comprehend the gravity of its skillful forces.

It was no longer a secret that this tactical foe's game plan was to defeat me by stealing my psychic playbook. At this point, it was obvious that I was clueless and powerless to devise a strategy that mitigated my vulnerabilities. This inability to quickly adapt was not only obvious, but it left me unquestionably in trouble, both on offense and defense. For the first time in my life, I felt mindlessly inept.

One of the earliest anxieties that I struggled with was grasping whether mental illness was a disease, an emotional behavior, or simply an incident induced by a trauma that forces one to withdraw from who one was in the past. I believe this infirmity subconsciously contributed to an imagery that was ever-changing. Because of my emotional changeability, my vision was unclear as to my illness, causing me to become blinded even by the sight of my reality. It conflicted with the way I was seen as well as the manner in which I viewed myself.

Usually, the sufferer does not visualize this frontal view because the distance of detectability is sometimes nearsighted and then can be suddenly farsighted. In theory, I could feel the impact of change because of the pain's internal proximity, but the ability to confirm the detriments was far off; it required confirmation from an external professional. At this point, my darkness was neither reflective nor subjective, although I believed it to be both. Some may suggest this was a type of hallucination, which is possible. However, it was my perceptive reality filled with layers and layers of personal fear that weighted both my exterior and interior posture. It devastated me in many ways. My existence was superficially becoming a skeletal statue.

I was in desperate need of aid to preclude further demise of my mind, body, and soul, which were crucial to my survival. This illness is an ongoing endemic, and its origin is debatable; nonetheless, I am not without an intimate acquaintance. Many of us either know or previously knew someone suffering from mental illness. As a mental illness sufferer, I needed to be heard, but I also needed support to be understood without being made fun of.

I believe that individuals suffering from mental illness may unconsciously become a enemies to their recovery. They feel such trepidation as to how much information they are willing to share so they can minimize or protect themselves from the cruelty of being labeled as *crazy*. Sufferers like me must decide daily who, what, where, when, and how our existence prevails within a society of slanted preconceptions.

Hello, strangers! I am a forty-eight-year-old African American woman, mother of three, wife for almost twenty years, military veteran, MBA graduate, and wounded warrior confronted by mental illness. My initial response was an adamant refusal to surrender to any diagnosis destined to steal my treasures of livelihood. This in no way means that I denied the diagnosis, but I did want to not own the prognosis that it was too difficult to overcome. There are other life-threatening illnesses like cancer where patients find themselves in the fight of their lives. Believe me, mental illness is no different. You must fight to win!

Initially, in my case, mental illness was not manageable until I became open to incorporating a strategic wellness plan. This plan addressed PTSD, severe depression, multiple anxieties, memory loss, and claustrophobia. One professional also diagnosed me as bipolar. It was critical for this wellness plan to be interconnected with widespread support, treatment, resources, and most importantly, the powers of my God.

My inside view varied from the perspective of many outside views, revealing how far apart the perspectives were. I suggest that people understand that an illness like mine was a result of various contributing incidents and not an inborn illness. An injury, illness, or traumatic event can change the directional path of one's insanity. I reject the opinions of most outsiders because of their presumption in labeling mental illness as the sufferer's defect caused by that individual. The behaviors and flawed perceptions of outsiders, even while contradictory, often involve perspectives that are inconclusive but also without merit.

I am not a professional doctor who diagnoses mental illness; I am sharing knowledge as a sufferer affected by detrimental experiences related to mental illness. The reality encircling mental illness is that who you are today may not be who you will be tomorrow. I imagined myself as a strong, independent, and competent warrior prior to the diagnosis, but now I am beginning to conceive a different set of strengths that are self-determining. The daily battle is to not fall prey to a relentless yet ghostly undistinguishable power whereby you become confused by the former you versus the current you.

Mental illness is complicated and not easy to express or share. The reason I am finally sharing firsthand experiences is to enlighten people as to the seriousness of mental illness. Few, if any, are willing to be a voice to express a panoramic view, divulging a 360-degree vulnerability circumference about self relating to mental illness. Frankly, none of my friends, associates, coworkers, and even some of my family knew anything of my mental health struggle because it was a closet of skeletons and all hush-hush. It was my little secret that I wanted to keep buried away in the dark. I shared my condition only with those I thought could comprehend the complexities involving my illness. You know, those people who *needed* to know, not those who *wanted* to know.

I believed that allowing too many ears and eyes of access might prove detrimental not only to my recovery but also to my reputation. This illness was so dark, and shining too much brightness on it was difficult for me. I had to decide the appropriateness of the lighting to release myself from this stealthy darkness. It was time to walk one step at a time, refuting mental illness because it was redirecting my directional purpose. I detoured, so let's journey through this encounter with complete openness.

Suddenly, I feel carefree about letting outsiders inside my world and giving them an opportunity to witness the altering of my emotions that was inflicted by mental illness. The beat is awkwardly annoying, yet so rhythmic, because I cannot pinpoint the composition to which my mind connects. Dancing, partying, and enjoying music are usually joyful events that allow the innocence of the soul and the mind to relish moments of love and happiness. However, this irregular yet offbeat tune is much too erratic.

Guarded mostly by fear, mental illness sufferers experience explosive and unpredictable uncertainties that seem to alternate between volcanic one minute and tornadic the next. It is difficult to pinpoint the eruption of mental illness as well the evolution and what exactly causes this interruption of mental stability. I witnessed the weather in Kansas City about six years ago undergo an unimaginable period of seasonal confusion. It rained, hailed, sleeted, and snowed all in the same day. That seems impossible, but much like mental illness, it involves the unpredictability of a change so sudden or erratic that is mind-boggling to process.

This stranger within is a real threat to myself, loved ones, bystanders, and caretakers. Certainly, it's not by choice, but a consequence of my mental state. Many of us think of strangers as passersby, onlookers, and spectators—not those we live with, like family and friends. But in my family, I am the stranger, and so too are they strangers to me. Frankly, our current interactions are no longer synchronized with the commonalities of our past that connectively harmonized our relationships.

I became emotionally detached, and yet I attached my future to my husband. After all, he is my best friend, lover, and partner—but still I saw him as only a familiar stranger. I only physically embraced him if my emotions permitted such an action; otherwise, I resisted the affection in hopes of avoiding his genuine probes of concern. It felt odd, but our marital relationship became passive in nature. We no longer connected as emotional partners but rather as spousal strangers with shared responsibilities. It was not because of desiring to separate or divorce, but because mental illness made me feel unloved, unwanted, and even more so undesired.

After feeling so emotionally depleted, I sought a psychological journey to discover myself all over again, or at least to rebirth the former me. I was unexpectedly led toward a void filled with mystery. It was important that I connected with this place of anonymity, so I converted into a zone of carefree thinking. It proved beneficial in the sense that my road to recovery was no longer narrow-minded but open, so I could experience expounded freedoms.

It was if I was being unleashed to explore the wilds of unchartered grounds—to find myself without a map or a clue. It was refreshing to take my first steps just to inhale the air of newness. I had no idea that I was asleep. Perhaps I was dreaming or hallucinating about this journey, but also a new day was upon me, which meant optimism was present.

Early this morning, I consciously introduced myself to me, as if to a withdrawn stranger awakening from a deep sleep to new yet unchanged discoveries. The discovery was that it was a new day, but I was still the timeworn mental illness sufferer. After a sleepless night of tossing and turning, my dreams were not filled with fantasies but realities that had thus far caused nothing but havoc in my life, both at sunrise and sunset. The havoc contributed to obscurities involving things that possibly reveal what issues, incidents, or emotions would trigger me to slip into a state of unconsciousness. In this state of cerebral suppression, I tolerated my strangeness to me as well as those nearby.

There were some very beautiful things that surrounded me and some very loving people, yet I searched to rediscover myself—to grasp the reasoning behind feeling irrelevant after contributing so much time and effort to building a life of relevance. I sat down on my large, comfy bed in admiration of colorful golden walls with shaggy carpet on the floor, a corner space with a white couch filled with square throw pillows, and a jewelry box filled with gems, diamonds, and gold that my husband had bought me during our nineteen years of marriage. As I sat there, I began to ponder my life and what had led me on this journey. I felt hopeless at times, but also hopeful that things would change. The room appeared so full of life but so bleak and hollow, with no emotional depth.

These feelings were a daily ritual, as if worshipping misery was something I preferred. The truth was, I did not know how to feel any better because I did not detect anything was wrong. I felt nauseous and weak, sensing a collapse at any time, although not sure of rising emotions spewing from my bodily roots. Nonetheless, I would soon comprehend the storms of emotions that my life was about to undergo: rain, sleet, and hail, all in interchanging seasons, with only a glimpse of sunshine to give me hope.

Mental illness is like a thief, robbing you of joy, happiness, and livelihood to be productive without requiring any measurement of functionality. The ability to function in a setting is sometimes the most difficult thing to do. The very superficial innocence of an unstable mental illness sufferer is made up of their surroundings, current incidents, or existing situations, which can lead to remembrance of episodes that trigger internal and emotional uproar.

The one thing I believe helped me to outwardly cope for years was the love and support of my spouse, Budd. He and I have shared so many memories of love and war, both on the battlefield as well as in our marriage. His love has always been my angelic protection, especially whenever I felt vulnerable and ill. He has never judged anything I have done or how I express myself. He always forgives and forgets with such tenderness.

Although his tenderness was constant, it was apparent that he, too, was beginning to suppose that not all was right. I would have major outbursts, going from zero to one hundred in a matter of seconds over the smallest of things. This was unusual, and I know for certain that it wasn't me but rather something or someone deep within dictating my emotions. Budd's glimpses at me became stares of wonder; however, most perplexing was that the smirks were about to become more frequent.

Budd would appear to look at me in awe after I returned from the war that we both had served in together for almost a year. He would visit me frequently at my combat location to offer love and help to stabilize my anticipated yet tense emotions. We were in combat, and numerous missions were not only dangerous but also life-threatening, especially for him. This fear and anxiety is unexplainable to most people since only about 1 percent of Americans volunteer to serve their country.

Most times, serving one's country results in being in a faraway land, surrounded by an imperceptible enemy. Amazingly, like other veterans, we made this ultimate sacrifice not realizing or considering the unforeseeable detriment that would impact us during later years of our lives. Surely my exposure to a faraway environment and its expectations was a contributor to my underlying sensitivities.

These internally brewing changes began to covertly weaken my core. After being away from my children and being subdued daily by an emotional roller coaster, something was bound to transmute. I suppose Budd had to consider even when I tried to suppress my emotions that something was changing in my expressive behavior. I believe this worrisome change in my ability to cope instigated more frequent visits than planned.

Looking back, Budd possibly saw an altering state of mind regarding my mental stability but refrained from sharing for months to protect us both from toxic perceptions. Putting others before self was always at the forefront, and because of our leadership positions, neither of us would ever jeopardize the safety of our comrades or the mission. As previously mentioned, to ridicule me and other mental illness sufferers is to render an injustice based on the misbelief that we ail only because we lack the strength to overcome and are receptive to being weak.

Leaders lead and followers accept their roles, although at times it is critical and cumbersome to do both simultaneously, especially in the military when enduring life-threatening situations. Those following your lead are attentive not only to what leaders verbalize but also what they competently exemplify. It was evidently conflicting and difficult to trust a leader who appeared unstable in such an environment—whether mentally or emotionally—and unable to make sound decisions. If a leader or subordinate appeared incapacitated, it undermined authority as well as competency.

Thus, concerns regarding individual sanity were not something I was willing to risk divulging to anyone. It's simple: warriors are seen as heroic, and therefore it is intolerable to suggest that they are not stable and sound. Expressing something so sensitive in nature would have been frowned upon by leaders and those I led. I had no choice but to suppress my fears and anxieties as I sought to be courageous in protecting and serving my obligations to our country.

Visualizing or experiencing circumstances where life was lost or injured during my stint in combat made me more resilient and determined to do everything possible to persevere and save my own life. While at war, my outlook about living intensified with a more profound perspective to cherish life. No one can object that life is the most priceless yet temporary gift bestowed upon humanity. Apprehensions were visibly reflected upon the faces of many comrades who boarded the Boeing 757 with me to go to war. This suggested a plane of fears but also the onset of comprehending the gravity of what being at war really meant, as well the aftermath that war produces: casualties amongst different ranks and of complex injurious natures.

After this long journey to a foreign land to risk my life along with the lives of my comrades, we landed amidst the winds of uncertainty. We convoyed through many dangerous towns and cities, hoping that, as projected by our leaders, this would be a quick in-and-out combat mission with no attack by the Iraqi enemy. We were en route to Mosul, as my company had been in Iraq for about sixty days. We had staged our equipment, vehicles, and personnel in a sandy desert area, awaiting command orders to move forward to the next location, when suddenly fear shook our home away from home territory.

Our peacekeeping endeavor suddenly yet unexpectedly turned into a combat encounter. Soldiers from our sister units had been attacked while on foot patrol. This was the beginning of my psychological fear. I recall this incident resulting in the first combat demise of a comrade. It undeniably shook and stirred emotions that I had never recognized or felt. As a soldier, it was difficult to process the visual of a dying peer. This horrific incident played over and over in my mind as I witnessed this courageous warrior fight for life while bleeding to death. It was then and still is now a haunting experience. It surely affected my psyche!

The details are far too graphic to describe, even to this day. I felt responsible for being incapable of prolonging the life of this dying soldier I had never met, which was indicative of the bond that service members share. It doesn't matter your race, religion, gender, or perspective, we all bleed the same blood. He was a severely wounded comrade who I later discovered was a newlywed and new father to a little girl.

I clearly remember the tags that lay on his blood-bursting chest as the doctors struggled to revive him and return the overwhelming amount of blood lost. It seemed the more blood they tried to restore in his debilitated body, the more rapidly the blood seeped out, gushing over the plastic-covered floors inside the makeshift surgical tent. Make no mistake based on the tent's outer shell: it was an amazing facility, comparable to a bona fide hospital operating room.

The situation was becoming more dire with each passing second. Soldiers who had the same blood type were summoned to donate blood because of his excessive bleed-out. No matter how desperately the doctors struggled to save him, however, it was no use. The soldier fighting for his life succumbed to the bullet wounds suffered while on foot patrol.

The room became silent, with emotional gestures of unspoken disappointment for not being able to save the wounded soldier. However, the poignant realization was that this incident was only the beginning of ensuring preparedness for future casualties. I stood numbed for minutes and soon thereafter returned to my cot in the back of my sleep tent. I was heartbroken for a reason that I was unable to share or admit during the unsuccessful efforts to save the soldier. As I tossed and turned, reliving the incident, I could not sleep. So I left the tent torn in so many pieces. This was the first time I had witnessed a death so up close and personal.

I walked around the small military secure area alone, trying to grapple with my emotions as well as rid my mind of this devastating visual of a dying and helpless warrior. I stumbled upon the psych team's medical tent area and noticed a light on and voices chattering about the trauma that had occurred in the surgery tent. At this point, it was about one o'clock in the morning. I entered the tent and joined the emotional discord of a loss.

There were four of us, but suddenly my release of remorse became overwhelming, making it obvious just how weepy I felt about the death of this soldier. I suppose at this point I was the only one other than the surgeons who knew that an important medical solution was requested but not available. Ultimately, I felt it was my responsibility to stock this vital item as a seasoned noncommissioned officer. In my opinion, my culpability was in failing to ensure that a product called blood coagulant was on hand. This is a product used during medical crisis for plasma loss. It is critical during surgeries if dealing with injuries with the possibility of massive blood loss.

I recalled inquiring whether I should request any blood coagulant with the first ground supplies, but it was refuted. Frankly, no one anticipated the unit having any casualties within the first thirty days after arriving in Iraq. Honestly, I blamed myself for such ill-preparedness, even though it was the top leader who rejected the request to purchase the item. I believed at that time, had I known the full scope of the product's life-saving purpose, my determination to obtain it might have persuaded the commander to ensure on-hand stock of the item. I cried and sobbed, realizing for the first time that we were at war and this was not an illusion.

The morning after the soldier's death, the surgeon spoke with me to assure me that there was nothing they could have done to preserve the soldier's life. The surgeon also comforted me with compassion, cautioning me not to blame myself, because it was by fate, not my failure. The surgeon also conveyed, based upon his professional experience, that the soldier's grave condition was unpromising for even his surgical mastery, but he had been hoping and praying for a miracle.

This traumatic incident haunted me for days, and now years have passed and it's still very painful. To add more stress to the situation, some unknown source had contacted the father of the fallen soldier, and the father had been covertly informed that his son had been killed. I could not believe how fast this news traveled stateside from a war zone. Coincidentally, when the father called the training operating center, I was the only one in the briefing tent, so I had no choice but to answer the phone. I had no idea it was the deceased soldier's father. My heart must have stopped beating, with a pause that lasted seconds but felt like minutes.

I could hear the father sobbing with panic as he tried to contain his emotions. It was clear that he knew it was true, yet he needed a confirmation that his worst nightmare had become a reality. It was so humanly difficult to be put in this position, burdened with dual liability for one family. I had failed to provide the coagulant, and now I had to converse with the father, to whom I had an implied duty to substantiate the soldier's death. My goal was to calm and console the father with kind and compassionate information without divulging the truth. I did not have authorization to confirm his son's death or answer most of his questions.

Two of the father's questions were: Can you tell me if my son was shot? and Where is my son receiving treatment? Heartbroken, with tears in my eyes, I stayed strong to avoid further panic. Quietly, I listened to the father's concerns. I convinced him that an authorized leader with more details would contact him to provide information regarding his son's injuries. I felt so caught in the middle with awkwardness, but I tried to be as poised as possible.

After experiencing a situation like this, for some odd reason the vision of losing life ignited my desire to birth new life, as if it would replace this soldier's life. It's hard to connect the analogy of death versus life in this instance. Ironically, the one thing that gave me hope and not despair during the remaining tenure of combat was the possibility of birthing another child—and hopefully a daughter, since I had two sons.

Budd and I really had discussed having another child after we returned from Iraq, but this was almost like a premonition in an unusual way that I too would die in one world but live again in another. I did not comprehend this journey of fate until many years later that some war-ridden trauma would pierce my body like a fiery bullet. Death would halt, and my life would be saved by a godly spirit, unlike my fallen comrade.

The soldier who lay upon the cold, still operating-room table had a picture of his daughter around his neck that was connected to his dog tags. I have never forgotten that painted image of a child who unknowingly had become fatherless and might never comprehend the courage of her father. I was told the wounded soldier talked about his daughter the entire time until he lapsed into unconsciousness. As a veteran, I am not certain whether the ultimate sacrifice of death is a commendable service for country or a contemptible one filled with heartbreaking memories that grief-stricken children must bear, causing the legacies of many service members to be shortened by a war that wounds uncertainly.

Chapter 2

Infiltration by an Innocent Stranger

L ife is as fragile as the shell of an egg that embraces the yolk, symbolizing the instability of an unknown existence. The existence is perhaps only tangible because of its concealed context, while the physicality or conditional health is indefinite. It is purely inconceivable that the egg may be diseased with a condition that perhaps goes undetected during pregnancy or even for many years to come. The unorthodox inference is that uncertainty is never with certainty because things can change unpredictably.

As a mom who birthed a few progenies, I was certainly concerned about the health of each burgeoning offspring, especially since they were precious gifts by God at varying milestones of my life. I was in my twenties for the first, thirties for the second, and forties with my last pregnancy. Nevertheless, it has been a complete joy to parent each of them. It is even more humbling to absorb the fact that God chose me to feed and nurture the life of not just one other soul but three.

The ability to parentally connect with a child—whether genetically, scientifically, or through advocacy—is one of the most heartfelt blessings imaginable. The mere fact that you are obligated to put the needs of someone else above your own interests, I believe, demonstrates one of the most sacrificial mannerisms of unconditional love: relinquishing selfishness. All of us are selfish at some point in our lives, even if only for a second. There is nothing wrong with being selfish if you recognize that your selfishness is without malice or detriment.

I believe that, from time to time, it is necessary to focus on self and not others. It is good to be selfish on occasion. If you always put everything and everyone before yourself, your place of worthiness may become devalued. People who fail to appreciate my kindness have often made me feel as though it was my fault, which made me feel taken for granted. That was hurtful. Every once in a blue moon, rotate your mind to make yourself more significant. Even the sun and the moon alternate their rotations of relevancy. That's why there is day and night, light and darkness.

Have you ever just held an egg in your hand and admired the imagery, imagining the miracle that is projected to be revealed? Just imagine for a moment that your life began in the same mystical context. All eggs are presumably innocent, with hope that life in its purest form is untainted. However, sometimes before or soon after the egg's breaching, an exactness of its condition is normally revealed. A thin-skinned egg is a fragile entity; therefore, we are taught to use caution when preparing to crack an egg to prevent the substance from a slimy spill.

Women understand the need to attend prenatal appointments at least once a month as a health benefit for themselves and their unborn child. The appointments become more frequent during the latter stages of pregnancy, unless there are earlier signs of complications. The physician's goal is to monitor the growth of this fertilized egg that is in a constant state of transformation, forecasting the delivery of a healthy child without adverse complications.

Oftentimes, when a human egg is deliverance-ready, it may symbolize the uncertainty of the infant's current situation but also offer insight into whether, as life progresses, there may be health concerns. An unpredictable impediment at any state can cause a progressive change, sparking immediate concern over some detected vulnerability. This metaphor characterizes my apprehension as to the strangeness of any egg's state of being until its exposure. Comprehending my state of mind and its shifting has generated interest in uncovering the beginning of my egg's fragility and whether it travels generationally.

My mom and dad were young teenagers when they married, and while coupling, they birthed four eggs. I jokingly mock to my siblings from time to time that not all our parents' eggs are productively equal. Some seemed to be different in ways that instigated much curiosity about the differences among these four eggs. It is obvious that although siblings grow up together, differences clearly exist. These differences are not just in shape, size, or physicality, but also the dimensional behavior of character and responsiveness to life's triumphs.

I am the middle sibling, and supposedly I am much like my father, who is a stranger in many aspects of life. My father was absent from my life in many ways after returning from the Vietnam War. Although, no pun intended, my father was around long enough to insert his sperm with good intentions, it was not like a sperm-bank donation but more like participation without presence because of mental illness versus a monetary incentive.

I personally believe that I am an egg of mystery. I was the first child born after my father's return from the Vietnam War, where evident changes were occurring too often in his display of erratic behaviors. As a veteran like my father, I can attest to the psychological and emotional traumas experienced during war. My father was wounded inside and out, and he had no one to turn to.

Some may refute the notion that society was a major contributor to the demise of many minorities' psychological stability. Countless minorities were drafted against their will to go to war and fight for the democracy of a foreign government when they themselves were not acknowledged or respected at home by their own American government. I can only imagine, and I still struggle with America's prejudiced society, where veterans risk so much to promote and sustain the freedoms of democracy on behalf of all people, regardless of creed, color, or nationality. A covert barrier is and was prevalent to objectify minorities after returning from Vietnam, which was an added layer of emotional rejection by a country and its people that my father was willing to die for.

This is not a disrespectful expression but an emphatic acknowledgement of the buried wounds of my father and the conception of my paternity. This stranger who is my father may have inadvertently donated impure genetics without any consideration to his own health or the health of future births. Inherited genetics is possibly an indicator that may have resulted in the implantation of mental illness encounters that added to my suffering. I do not now nor will I ever penalize my father for his contributions, because without his voluntary seed contribution, I would not exist.

Again, all eggs are innocent until fissure lines develop, causing an interruptive imbalance between sanity and insanity. So who do you blame? Is it hereditary, self-induced, or the societal woes of life? These questions have riddled my brain and emotions for the past five years, so it is time to face them head-on. I believe this opposition is one of the most mystifying yet therapeutic journeys. My privation is to rid myself of being an indeterminate mental illness sufferer.

I am not skeptical surrounding the illnesses, but I am very unsure of the origin. The skepticism surrounding anything is what I believe can afflict the mind, which resulted in me questioning my own state of mind even in a comatose existence. Since my birth decades ago, it seemed, I started to experience instances of unpredictability that were noticeable as an adult. I was not sure if I or my mom had missed early signs during my adolescent years, so I began assessing my own emerged eggs even closer. It is possible that, based upon my experiences as a teen, that some incidents caused me to become depressed and anxious, especially surrounding sports and strict disciplining by my mom. I prayed by the warm embrace connecting my eggs to my womb that my children had not been genetically wounded by the instabilities of their mom.

I have had the awesome privilege to birth three eggs thus far in my lifetime; God knows I pray no more are in my future. Not only was each of my perfect eggs different, but each was dynamic in his or her own way, revealing different complications. Metaphorically speaking, my gestational beginning from an egg to adulthood was perhaps infused with a yoke of unpredictability. My effort was to safeguard and protect each of my eggs from external or internal havoc, impeding their complete development.

The first pregnancy produced an array of issues, including depression, and I gained over one hundred pounds. Clearly, I was unhealthy in a myriad of ways that produced even more concerns for my psychological health. The second egg's birth was the healthiest; I gained only about forty-five pounds, but I suffered three minor strokes. There were visible effects, but perhaps some lurking. The delivery of my third egg was the beginning of a sweltering encounter fueled by uncertainties. These ambiguities seemingly encompassed mental illness, causing a volcanic eruption and spilling into crevices that are yet in healing.

My first egg was an inspiration to be successful. My second egg was one of motivation. My third egg is the one of devotion that ultimately encouraged me to acknowledge that mental illness was not a ruse but my reality. I often was seeing life through broken lenses that were tinted with the haze of fuzzy darkness. This third egg was embedded in my womb at the ripe age of forty-two, an age that most consider to be too old or premenopausal to conceive a child. I had in no way planned this pregnancy, but I will forever be thankful for its implantation.

To be frank, my husband and I had discussed the possibility of having a tubal ligation, since I had not become pregnant after praying for a daughter for over eight years. I had relented and was psychologically moving forward. No more babies! Have you ever wanted something so bad but it did not come to fruition? I began to focus my energies on something else, like work. I had worked so hard throughout my career and had finally started to gain traction in achieving the goals I set. This was a time in my life when I felt confident in my stance from all angles. I was very engaged in my career; in fact, I was about to be awarded a command position to lead an organization. I had dreamed of an opportunity like this for many years.

I made a drastic change in my career when I transitioned from enlisted to the officer ranks. I had grown so much as a leader after the war in Iraq that my military ambition was to command troops. The decision to tap into this dream was not necessarily voluntarily at the time, but it was mandated by the will of a negative foe who I was at odds with over an issue that I prefer not to disclose to protect those I do not have to share. Nevertheless, General Petraeus, who was an angel in disguise, gave me an opportunity believed impossible by many of my foes.

Soldiers exemplify a level of pride in who they are and what they represent that may be inconceivable to some. This job opportunity I was about to be granted made me so proud of my attainments, yet so afraid of what the job required. My nervousness led to stress over the need to show that I was the right candidate and no hesitation should even be considered.

To my surprise, days before the boss's decision to announce his choice for the job, I became very ill. I was so wracked with illness that I lay in bed and could not even lift myself to go from one room to the next. I was weak and dizzy, and I felt so unlike myself. After a day of this sickness, I asked my husband to take my blood pressure. It was so low that I should have been at a hospital, but I brushed it off.

Suddenly, I thought to ask my husband to go to the store to get a pregnancy test—at least two of them. I do not recall if I had missed my period, since I had been so enthralled with work and the new opportunity that I was about to gain. However, this was an unusual feeling, and the only time I recalled feeling this odd was when I became pregnant. I had not taken any type of birth control pill in eight years because I wanted badly to conceive a child.

I was not expecting to be pregnant, but I wanted some mental clearance that whatever it was, it would soon pass. Since my husband was to get two different brands of pregnancy test, my intent was to have a first and second confirmation. Hence, I took both tests, one around noon and the other before going to bed. Happily, both tests were negative, but that made me feel even more edgy. I assumed that my body was experiencing some type of infection, virus, or stress-related incident.

The next morning, I felt fine. The test had revealed that I was egg-womb free, so I went to work. The workday was calm, even though I was conducting inventories to assume my new position. My womanly intuition signaled me that my queasy body was out of tune, so I needed to go to the doctor. I called my husband and had him meet me at the medical facility to have some blood work done. Once the tests were completed, we waited to see if some medical explanation could be provided—especially since my medical history included a minimum of three TIAs (minor strokes) determined by previous doctors.

Suddenly, the technician reappeared with a smile and stated that they had found the root and the main cause of my symptoms. I replied, "What is it?"

"You are pregnant!" the technician replied.

My husband and I looked at each other, and shock waves ran through my body while a big smile filled the handsome face of my husband. I was simply speechless. I thought, *Oh my God! I am forty-two, old as dirt, about to take command, and how will this news transfer to my supervisors in viewing my competency?* After all, I was the chosen candidate for the position over two other highly qualified professionals. I even surmised that one of the rejected candidates would be fuming, since he really felt slighted because of his seniority.

Once we returned home, I cried, sniffling the sentiment, "Why me?" The timing could not be more dreadful. I refused to share the news with anyone for weeks, including my two other children, who were seventeen and ten at the time. The reason for not sharing this miracle was because I wasn't certain whether this was a blessing or curse. I was allowing myself to feel cheated out of an opportunity. This was not the image of life, success, or career fulfillment that I had envisioned.

I beat myself up emotionally, wondering whether to abort this growing egg. I thought about this unexpected pregnancy for a couple of weeks and told my husband that I wanted to abort the child. I just was not ready to parent another child. I was afraid that it would complicate our lives in ways that were unthinkable. My husband was not happy about my abortion intention, but he was very supportive.

My husband had to go out of town for his job for a week, so I was left all alone to contemplate options and weigh the outcome of my choices. Years prior to this pregnancy, my youngest son had asked me repeatedly to have another child because he wanted to be a "big brother."

I was like, "You have cousins; plus, try to enjoy being Mommy's little baby." This apparently soothed his sibling fantasies to be enthroned as an elder brother, so he agreed.

I was at a standstill with my decision. I would call my husband, crying and asking him what I should do. He never once scolded or demeaned me for my emotions and indecisiveness. Surprisingly, my husband was the one who made the appointment for me to go to have the procedure at an abortion clinic. My husband and I sat and discussed me being pregnant numerous times, and his support was evident. He would stare into my eyes with love and compassion.

I recall him telling me on more than one occasion, "Honey, it is your decision. Although I am the father, it's a choice that lies mostly in your hands." It was comforting that he trusted me to do what was best. Deep down, he probably knew more than me that I was not going to go through with the abortion.

Budd had planned to be there throughout the entire process. The closer the appointment came, the more conflicted I became. I was beginning to worry whether anyone at work would discover the pregnancy that I was not only aiming to keep a secret but also aiming to abort. Two days before the abortion appointment, my husband and I were riding through our neighborhood, noticeably cruising past a school-daycare, and the conversation came up. My husband asked if I was okay, and if this was something I really wanted to do for the sake of my career.

Suddenly, that "aha moment" flashed. I remembered not only what my husband said but also the prayer I had prayed eight years earlier. My selfishness plummeted at the thought of terminating a gift that other women desperately yearned for—to be pregnant. How self-regarding was I? It would be would foolish to rid my body of something that was a part of me and a man who I loved so much.

I looked at my husband and whispered, "No job is more important than this pregnancy, and just maybe that position was not meant for me." God had an even bigger, more meaningful reward that would serve a different purpose to my very being. I was now six weeks pregnant and ready to reveal to the world that I was old but I still got it and was proud to be a mom carrying a third egg. First to get the news were our two sons, and we did not know what to expect. I began to conceptually prepare the scenario in which we would break this blissful news.

It was a Friday night after an exhausting week of work and trying to come to terms with the pregnancy. We decided it was the right time to tell the kids. To be honest, I was not excited, but more or less hesitant as to what to expect from the boys' response. It had been a long time since we'd had a baby around, and kids sometimes become selfish in desiring all the attention, with an unwillingness to share my time. My husband and I asked the kids to join us in the family room, where we usually watched television on a large, plush sectional. The kitchen was nearby; my husband had just finished cooking a pot of delicious gumbo. I was craving a hefty bowl, enticed by the aromas from one of my favorite Creole foods. I couldn't wait to eat!

Hunger was on my mind, but I knew something important took precedence over feeding my taste buds. A food like gumbo has to simmer, so we had time on our hands. We wanted to deliver the news gently, with responsive anticipation of their projected reactions. I loved and valued my children, so it was important to break the news in a more sentimental manner than abruptly saying, "I am pregnant!" I looked over at my husband and motioned for him to join me as I called the boys from their bedrooms, where they most likely were competing in a PlayStation game.

The room was dimly lit, with lighting from the television and kitchen beaming as the children ran down from upstairs. They rushed over to see what the call for them was all about. We rarely called them both simultaneously. Even they knew this was unusual, so it must be something important. My oldest son, Parriz, had a serious look on his face; the youngest son, Jostein, was just afraid he had done something wrong.

I sat in the middle of the couch with my husband to my right, the youngest to my left, and the eldest to the youngest son's left. I begin to tell them that I loved them so much, and our family was about to experience a major event that would change our lives very soon and forever. My children probably thought this meant that Mom was about to redeploy to Iraq or somewhere. The boys looked at each other and then me and shouted, "What's wrong? Is everything okay?"

I told them to try to guess, but Parriz responded, "I'm not in the mood. Just tell us."

I could see fear creeping into their faces, so I quickly had to spit out the news: "We are going to have a baby!"

The room went silent. Our eldest son, who was a senior in high school, said, "What?" What did you just say?"

I repeated the words to make sure I was clear. "I am pregnant, and I am almost nine weeks."

He was speechless, and he didn't seem too cheery about this notion of another baby. Parriz was commonly not afraid to share his perspectives.

Meanwhile, the youngest child, Jostein, jumped to his feet and started to cry with emotion. He scared us, and I thought, *Oh my gosh, what have we done? This is not good or what we expected.* Suddenly, he screamed, "I am so happy! I cannot wait to be a big brother!" I was so relieved that at least one of our sons was happy. Honestly, it is hard to satisfy everyone with life's choices, but we often try.

I hugged Jostein so tightly. Possibly this was one of the confirmations I needed, which was for the children to be accepting and happy. I was still baffled by Parriz's reaction, since he was an egg that was ready to be de-nested. Hopefully, the eldest egg would take notice of his brother's display of nestling harmony so that he could share and make room in the love nest.

The next big reveal was to go to work and share the news with my superior. Although I worked with him daily, I did not know what to expect. I did anticipate that his response would not be accommodating, and perhaps he would be disappointed. The lieutenant colonel's consternation, in my opinion, would be based upon the inability to have me available to do jobs that others could not do or he did not trust to do. This senior officer was overly reliant upon my high-level work and labeled my work once as "Everything you touch turns to gold!" That was high esteem for my work performance.

The one good thing I hoped for was that since the lieutenant colonel had a son he adored and often talked about with such pride, he would understand. After all, the two of us had a great work relationship—I was no doubt one of his top performers—so I expected his approval or at least his support. I also believed that he had somewhat of a fascination with my tendency to get things done without delay, which was deemed a necessary attribute of an accomplished military officer.

I arrived at my superior's office and approached him slowly as he sat behind this huge desk, which faced the entryway to his office. He had an unusual look on his face, especially since he had asked me to report to his office. This request felt odd, because my initial intent was to ask if I could speak with him about my all-too-important issue.

He asked me to sit at a round table across from him, and he proceeded to discuss the newly assigned position. The discussion revealed that even though I was expected to take command of a company in about three weeks, the plan had changed, with unmerited implications. My news could wait, because yet another confirmation had to be revealed.

My boss appeared nervous, with somewhat of a somber mood. Initially, he spoke softly, as if the news I was about to receive from him was as shocking as my protected egg secret. Gradually he stated, "A new boss has arrived, and his command prerequisites are different from those of the previous boss."

At first, I did not comprehend what direction he was going with this statement. Gazing into my eyes, he murmured, "You will not be able to command the position that was promised as well as earned!" It was because of the changes directed by a higher echelon of authority. I was shocked and saddened, desperately wanting to release some type of emotion, but what? In the military, I was taught discipline and required to maintain professional composure when speaking with someone of high authority.

My initial reaction was shock and emotional discord. I could not think straight or focus on anything except proving them wrong and me right. Nonetheless, I did ask about the decision and initially tried to contest the pronouncement for a few days, based on how unfair it was. It was supposedly because I had not attended an eight-week course to certify one aspect of a position, even though I had demonstrated a wealth of experience, knowledge, and competency in so many other areas. I had worked so hard to command, and to have an opportunity to realize a twenty-year dream snatched away left me broken into pieces, with no peace of serenity. I had no answers, only questions.

Furthermore, I knew no one could ever provide professional or personal closure regarding this change. This was like a double whammy; how do you bounce back? The alternatives were, I could give up or give in, and so I gave in. Failure is not part of my DNA. I saw this obstacle as an opportunity to refocus; subsequently, I became optimistic and looked forward.

The time had come to cease my efforts to avoid unnecessary backlash for fighting for something I so desperately deserved and wanted. The reasoning was comparable to comprehending the realism sandwiched between birth and death—death of a career promotion or birth of a cherished egg lying deep within my womb. I walked to the bathroom and began to ruminate about how my life had changed in a matter of months. I gazed into a large mirror attached to the wall to stare with wonder. I undressed my covered belly, and at this very moment, I understood that I needed to release this career craze. Suddenly, I could focus on the upcoming release party to celebrate a new life.

Three days later, I returned to my superior's office to share the news. I explained to him that even though I was disappointed by the change in policy, I accepted it because it was not my career journey. I expressed cheerfully, "Sir, besides, I found out some great news that I want to share."

He smiled and said, "What is it?"

"I am pregnant, and I could not be happier. I prayed for this miracle for a long time, and finally God's blessing has been granted."

He was shocked but appeared to be happy for me. I believe he wanted me to serve in the position as much as I yearned to, but it was out of his control. We both felt like a major burden had been lifted, and no resentment was apparent on either one of our parts. I saluted him and walked toward the exit feeling no regret but the fulfillment of joy.

Just imagine: if I had aborted one of the most precious gifts imaginable and then the job was annulled as a matter of policy change, my regrets might have led to an emotional deflation that I often ponder. The newly revised policies surrounding the job made me unqualified based upon one certificate of completion, even though I had ten-plus years more experience than a majority of all those selected to serve in the position. Ironically, I was aiming to change an outcome that had already been predestined.

However, this change in decision presented underlying inferences that would entail many discussions linking my sudden pregnancy with the possibility of a job relocation. I did not foresee this incident sparking a change in my life, career, and, yes, mental healthiness. Unfortunately, the news release was out: "Pregnant with no job!" This had become my reality in a matter of days. I was still, of course, employed as a military member, but the option for job preference was modified based upon organizational demands. Therefore, I could not revert to my old job because of my promotion in ranking authority, as well allocation to fulfill a specific job position. This was an instance where rank dictated job specifications to assign personnel based upon the needs of the military, not the desires of oneself.

The most disappointing reciprocation of my work performance reimbursed minimal exchange for the value of my currency over a span of three years. I did not comprehend how impactful this change would become, producing an inability to market myself because of my pregnancy. My worth and relevancy had simply diminished. Women who suffer from this temporary yet natural malady are denigrated because of the stereotypical assumptions that job performance will decline. This incident helped me to gain an insight that perhaps is one of the most memorable and greatest lessons in life: everyone has a relevant perspective, but not everyone stands in a position of relevancy. Pregnant women are oftentimes seen as eccentric through the eyes of a stranger because the position we stand in is strange.

I became the oddball in the room not because I was a pregnant or an incompetent warrior but simply because of the judgment of strangers who reprimanded me, like other female soldiers, by supporting insensitive stereotypes about being pregnant. Whenever pregnant soldiers have medical appointments, inconsiderate leaders view it as an issue that impinges upon the success of the mission. In some instances, pregnant soldiers are expected to perform at the same level as they did prior to becoming pregnant.

While serving in the military many years after birthing my first two children, I had only six weeks to lose the pregnancy weight as well be prepared to take a physical fitness test. This was ridiculous, but many female soldiers had no choice but to comply. This is possibly due to a lack of educational awareness surrounding women's health when unaffected counterparts author policies that encumber post-partum healing and recovery. During the first two deliveries, I gave up bonding time with my infant and suffered torn stitches from giving birth just so I could comply with military standards.

Many of my coworkers lacked the empathy to realize that I

stood in the same position as many of their wives, sisters, and one day perhaps their daughters. The lack of compassion demonstrated by most of my peers was hard for me to digest. It was difficult to comprehend; thus, I always gave a 100 percent unyielding effort no matter what. In fact, it was likely the opinionated bias displayed on their faces that made me desire seclusion away from the workplace. I suppose their responses were what I feared most—them conversing on their perspectives about me being pregnant at my age.

Well, I did not have to search or wait for such responses any longer, even if they were not verbalized. The soundless responses were very apparent, but soon I became numb to them. I had to decide on the relevance of my own opinion, not so much the spectator's opinion; after all, it is my life, not theirs. Bystanders—men as well as other women, which is ridiculous—must not be so judgmental regarding medical symptoms that briefly modify the performance of a coworker, regardless of whether the condition is temporary or enduring. I was not openly ridiculed, but sometimes the stares, whispers, and unwanted opinions became awkward and annoying.

I remember being very ill one day with a headache that would not subside no matter what I did. The headache felt unusual, with blurry vision and a ringing in my ears that would not go away. I decided it was important to get checked out if it persisted, so I informed my boss as to what I was experiencing. I told him I was going to go to the neurology clinic, since my previous medical history was of major concern. Pregnancy at my age surely added a layer of worry.

My boss said, "Are you sure you need to, or is it just a pretense to leave work?"

I replied, "Yes, I need to!"

Although these were not the exact words he uttered, his expression spoke volumes as to his twisted perspective. Those superior to us feel elitist and often use different words to confuse rather than to clarify, which makes me ponder whether my pain was only superficial. Going forward, I decided not to acknowledge any external perceptions regarding my health unless they involved professional triage.

Soon thereafter, I learned that I was indeed being transferred to another local position that was about fifty feet away from the current position. I was not disappointed, because I was again collaborating with someone I not only enjoyed, but the two-way respect was evident. My transfer supervisor was a tall, white gentlemen who was just as surprised as I was by the change. However, he was also ecstatic that I had been transferred to work with him once again.

I learned that he had specifically asked that I come to work on his team. Frankly, everyone wanted a performer like me on their team, but there was just not enough of me to go around. I am not being self-centered; I am just very confident in what I do, and I provide competent work as an associate. Once you understand the difference between the two, it allows widespread recognition of your value, because your worth is literally your soul's commodity.

Chapter 3

Shades of Strangers

I was about twelve weeks along with this fertilized egg, which made me feel weird. This was my third pregnancy, but it was dissimilar to the other two pregnancies. This birth seemed to induce health crises far more in-depth, causing multiple emotions and behaviors. My emotions were changing, and it was not just the usual hormonal episodes of mood swings or swinging moods.

I noticed that things looked different not just by appearance but by my response to the illusions of what had appeared right before my eyes. The room was spinning like I had just jumped onto a merry-go-round, but of course few if any pregnant women would get onto such a ride during pregnancy. I must be dreaming!

I awakened to find myself sitting at my work desk as people walked by with muttering voices. Even though I was pregnant, I could not believe that I had fallen into unconsciousness at work, seemingly in a world far away. This episode of oblivion possibly meant that I was not asleep but insensible.

Soon thereafter, awakening from borders unknown, my mental vacation brought ire. Being asleep is one thing, but being unaware is another. It was just like having a dream where I remembered details, but this delusion felt more like hallucinating, with detachment from reality. Shortly after I came to my wits, my new supervisor beckoned me to his office. He proceeded to give directives and plans of operations for the next several days as I took detailed notes.

My supervisor often bragged on me to everyone, referencing attributes like dependability, reliability, collaboration, and keen mission forecast. I can promise you, this day was a rarity, and nothing was gold but instead sprinkled soot. I returned to my desk with the notes, but unfortunately, I could not understand anything on the paper; it was all scribbly and confusing. I grabbed the notepad, ran to my car, and sat there in disbelief as the tears started to pour from my eyes. I cried uncontrollably for almost thirty minutes.

I was crying because I was clearly confused, but my comprehension as to what had happened was vague. The good thing was that it was during my usual lunch break, so no one suspected anything with my absence from the office. This brief stint allowed me to break away from workplace normalcy and military operations.

I often sat in my car to escape the incredibly busyness of the mission office, gather my thoughts, and quite frankly exhale from all the inhalation of mission exhaustion. This job was an absolute terror for many; only a few could execute such a demanding workload that was continuously so brutal on the mind. I was finding it hard to focus the way I did earlier in my military career. The directives were given, but my mental lapse caused me to fail at accurately recording specific details.

Loss of details are not a good sign in any job, but in the military it is like compounding cataclysms to catastrophe. I had no way to retrieve the specific information without frankly admitting that I had experienced a mental blackout, not only to my leader but to myself. Either way, this was a lethal blow to my career. This made my situation even more difficult to share, so I continued grappling within.

I had become a stranger to myself, with an estranged emotional disconnect as to who I was. I knew my name, but I did not know who the name embodied. This was not a good sign! I did not know nor could I explain what was going on, but clearly something was wrong. I was not sure if it was my health failing or the pregnancy. Perhaps I was afraid to acknowledge either.

I returned from lunch to try to gain insight as to what my duties were for upcoming missions, but I made every attempt to stay clear of my supervisor. I did not want to disappoint him or let anyone know what was going on, because not only was the job demanding but I was now pregnant. A pregnant old lady is under more scrutiny than ever. I very well knew the stereotypes regarding pregnant women in the workplace. I would never, pregnant or not, give in to this fallacy to allow people to poker-chip my capabilities or my ambitions.

In my previous job, I was the only female out of eight people, the only mother and wife, but always the worker who stayed later than anyone else. Truthfully, I refused to be muted in light of my gender. I no doubt far exceeded the competency and performance of each of my counterparts. No matter how poised and capable I was at work prior to my recent ailments, however, my present did not reflect my past. I needed answers, and I was on a mission to find out what was transpiring.

I made an appointment at the hospital's neurology clinic so that I could be evaluated to assess the symptoms that I was experiencing. As stated earlier, I had suffered from a minimum of three TIAs, and the effects are sometimes not initially apparent but discovered because of later effects. The neurologist took several tests which went on for about an hour and then informed me of a pre-diagnosis: my memory was impaired, and I was at risk of a possible aneurysm and future stroke. This diagnosis led to me being put on immediate bed rest, fearing medical complications from my injurious past. The possibility of life-threatening complications was of serious concern.

I had noticed a few days prior that my headaches were becoming unbearable. The headaches had, without consent, overlapped the ringing and tingling in my ears, causing my vision to erupt into darkness. This was a double whammy: my past illness coupled with my present diagnosis. I had never experienced anything like this.

The doctor also advised that I was now a high-risk pregnancy because of earlier medical conditions, expressing concern that a brain aneurysm could be a possibility. Oh my gosh! I was silently filled with panic and bewilderment, trying to withhold my emotions. I did not want to show any signs of vulnerability. That is one thing that warriors never display, no matter what. When in the presence of others, no one should see you sweat.

I was so consumed with this news that I could not even bring myself to return to work to deliver it to anyone, let alone my superior. The fear was that the disappointment I was about to reveal would perhaps, in others' mind, validate male beliefs that women are not equal in the workplace because of the very natural gift of being pregnant and all its indeterminate complications. Since the neurologist had put me on bed rest for the next thirty days, I digitally scanned the document and sent it to my supervisor rather than return to the office.

Suddenly, I remembered that I had nothing to be ashamed or embarrassed about because not only was I an excellent performer at work, I had carried my other two eggs while working extensive hours. During my past two pregnancies, I went into labor while I was at work. I remember being nervous after being told by the nurse that I had already dilated two to three centimeters upon my arrival to the labor and delivery room.

This beloved egg was presenting some unusual challenges in my life and seemingly demanding complete devotion. This life God was about to bless me with commanded my full attention, regardless of my career or the expectations promoted by other people. I was precipitously pushed to the forefront of my own life to save another life … that nameless egg that Bud and I had prayed for and created. It is sometimes an insensitive expectation when people require your life to take a backseat as you sit in the driver's seat, chauffeuring your own journeys. For some reason, people do not realize that unsolicited advice delays awareness of where an individual is destined to go. Not all passengers understand that the fee for the privilege of riding along does not entitle them to give driving advice.

People from my workplace wanted me to continue performing

work at home even though I was on bed rest. My husband had to finally express to my boss that I was either resting, relaxing, or following the doctor's orders, which was to stay stress-free. They never realized that if you followed their paths and not yours, their weighted directives would deplete your energies and your ability to travel to your own desired destination. I just could not accommodate these demands that risked my health and the health of my unborn egg.

I had many supervisors and leaders throughout my career, and one thing for sure is that I never proclaimed myself to be perfect, but I was a reliable perfectionist. I do not ever recall a supervisor having to scold me or conduct a performance counsel regarding ineptitude in a mission or task. I took my job and my duties very seriously, and I understood the concept of carrying my load no matter the consequences.

There were times when I had to work extensive hours, perform tasks that were not in my job description, and sacrifice family time, all for the sake of accommodating the requests of other people while proudly serving my country. The military is a job like no other, because for those who enlist, the oath of service reigns supreme over everything and everyone. There were instances where I sometimes had unspoken obligations that I was unaware of. Either the obligation was imposed by someone else or failed by someone else, resulting in the calling in of my capabilities to rescue numerous failing missions. In other words, I was discreetly selected without knowledge of being the "chosen one."

I had no choice but to concur or risk failure. In these situations, the soldier becomes the loser and the overall unit loses too. It was difficult to satisfy the demands of a 24/7 job while stabilizing a 24/7 home front. The risk of not securing my own nestling of eggs was constant, but I am grateful that I managed to build a strong nest to hold them tightly as I career-hopped from duty station to duty station. Now I needed that same level of compassionate support that I had provided so many times before, but I do not believe it was benevolently extended. I sometimes wonder if I did something to contribute to this lack of empathy, but thus far I am blurred. It started to at tear at my emotions while ripping the camouflage of covering that exposed an emotionally injured warrior.

My face looked different. My weight was expanding, and my mood swings were in disarray. It was easy to accept myself as a stranger with whom I was unacquainted. My face aged with illness, my eyes were baggy from sleep deprivation, and I required additional hydration to energize my movements. I am sure the pregnancy contributed to some of these changes, especially the weight gain and mood swings, but I am not too sure regarding my irrational responsiveness.

The first time that I became faced with GEMS—an acronym I devised for Galvanizing to Eradicate Mental-Illness Silence—I fell deep into a depression in which I felt numbed toward society, my family, but especially my emotional clarity. I gave my illness the name GEMS because of the closeness I felt to this demonic foe. I was sobbing, and I wanted to keep my emotions hidden from everyone.

I sobbed in a rage because I knew I had lost complete control of who I was, and this instigated anger, even though I felt helpless. It was early in the evening, around six o'clock, and I sat in my bedroom feeling abandoned. The only safe refuge I could imagine was the closet in my bedroom, which provided an immediate escape. When I walked into the closet, I immediately felt safe, relieved, and in a place where I could encage myself as I struggled to cope psychologically. The emotions that were traveling through my lifeless carcass made me feel breathless.

I stayed in the closet for hours weeping, balled into one fearful explosive as a scared-stiff mother who knew this was unexplainable. Suddenly, I heard footsteps enter the room, and I quickly started to wipe away the tears. My husband entered the closet as I sat in this comfortable recliner that I had placed in the closet months earlier. He asked me why was I sitting in the closet. I started to scream and yelled, "Get out! Leave me alone!" My reaction frightened Budd because he was attuned to the person he was witnessing.

I continued to yell until he went away. It was clear that although he left the closet, he had not left the room. I was screaming to get immediate compliance to my demand that he leave me alone. I knew my husband did not like loudness, nor was he confrontational. Budd and I both were puzzled by emotional complexities. My secret was no longer captive in my mind; now my husband knew! I did not know how or perhaps even if I should share these episodes.

Undoubtedly, the man I loved was shocked by my reaction and perhaps feared being mauled. He is usually a very easy-going, considerate man, but my emotions were just too intimate to release to anyone. On one occasion, I attacked a family member with a bucket of paint. I threw a bucket of paint, hitting this person in the mouth, causing blood to pour from mouth, teeth, and gums. Twenty-seven stitches were sutured into this person's facial area. The good news was that despite some very understandable anger, the family member didn't want to press charges and have me jailed. It was clear that I suffered from severe claustrophobia and if locked up, might seek suicide to free myself, as with a case in Texas a few years past. A mental illness sufferer like me may find it too difficult to be imprisoned, both mentally and physically, because emotionally it is far too much captivity to digest.

Soon after my husband left the room, my sons entered the closet to see what was going on. I was unresponsive; I just stared with confusion as they both kneeled next to me, grabbing my hands to reassure me with hugs. I recall them both saying, "We love you." and "What's wrong? Please come out the closet!" I just couldn't, even though the most treasured three men who I breathed for had peacefully asked me to.

It was apparent that GEMS had a stronger hold on me than I had imagined. I sat in the closet for hours. It was almost midnight, and yet I had no ability to be courageous enough to exit this room of darkness. Finally, my family asked if I wanted to talk to Burroni. They would call her whenever things concerned them or cluelessness plagued their understanding of me during unusual times—whenever I needed a true friend.

My supernatural twin, Burroni is often referred to as my

mini-me. I call her and only her when I need a friend or confidante to offer candid advice. I am not afraid to hear anything she says because she is my equal in so many facets, and our friendship is based upon the rule of reciprocation: I give what I expect but I do not expect what I give. Let's face it, families are often not as connected or supportive as they should or profess to be. Plus, they often use your secrets as ransom, reminiscing inequities that seem coercive when you resist their demands like borrowing money or favors that you would rather avoid.

My eldest son, Parriz, telephoned my sister-mate, Burroni, and her voice alone provided something that no other voice gave me: pure serenity to let go, allowing comfort to flow into this darkened space. Burroni whispered, "I am here for you. Tell me what I can do to make you feel better." She asked my family to leave the dim closet so that we could be alone. It was almost as if I was secretly cheating on my family with a relationship that I so desperately yearned for, almost like a love affair.

No, we are in no way a fetish with each other; we share a sisterly bond that is filled with generous, unconditional nurturing and the most wholesome expressions of love. I smiled with joy because my BFF was there to comfort my weary soul. Her essence filled the closeness of this small closet, expanding her reach as she touched me with deep compassion. It felt like the closet space widened, even with draped clothing on each side and countless shoes stacked to the ceiling. Her presence was just that massive, and it became apparent that three was a crowd. I was in the closet suffering from an unknown ailment, my BFF was apparent even though by phone, and of course GEMS, my psychological foe, was still present, though mockingly silent.

GEMS had gained a foothold in my psychotic thinking, but now that Burroni had arrived, I was hoping she could make sense of something that I had no inkling of. The awkward meeting with us three in an unfamiliar setting was frightful in the least. It was emotionally suffocating. I had to determine what or how much I could reveal so that I could feel not only safe in my friendship with

Burroni but saved from the foe of GEMS, which had enrapturing control over my consciousness. I was wrapped and tangled in a web of dysfunction that hypnotized my capacity to process my emotional state of mind.

What is difficult to comprehend is that I had grown to love GEMS just as much as I had any family member. Odd, but true. Although GEMS was fleshless, it provided something sacred, allowing me to be emotionally vulnerable even at the jeopardy of my own emotions. Love is a strange emotion, and you never know who or why you become infatuated with someone or something until you find yourself out of your depth.

Chapter 4

Rivalry Amongst Strangers: Friend and Foe

E very love is initially strange, introducing a new feeling, emotion, thought, or just an interest to interact. Not all love is intimate love. Certainly this love in the closet was not my preferred type of intimacy, but it was a love of mystified confidence, an emotional invasion without sanction. Unlike my BFF Burroni, who was permitted to infiltrate this darkened world to offer wholesome sustenance, GEMS had invaded my consciousness without my consent. Burroni's intent was to subvert the power of this dangerous foe from within my spirit.

It may sound unusual to hear me say that I had strong feelings for GEMS just as I did for Burroni. GEMS had become a valued commodity that I believe coined my emotions from worthiness to worthlessness. It may be easier to understand just how controlling GEMS was if you have ever been in an unhealthy relationship. The emotions can be calm one instant and tornadic the next.

The truth of the matter was that I adored them both. They each provided something that I needed during capricious times. They were both trusted confidants who would never betray me and shared my most guarded fears of my mental illness. GEMS and Burroni could persuade me to release my feelings at any given time, offering an escape that freed me from myself.

It is known, even if rarely accepted, that one can be one's own worst enemy. This stranger from within was yearning to experience freedom. The isolated despair was my reality, and it had locked me into a secluded place that no one besides GEMS and I knew or was even conversant in. I was truly ecstatic that finally, another personality had invaded this saucy rumba for two by pardoning GEMS with a tap of release to let go of this emotional constraint, even if only for a second or two.

Although I adored these two, Burroni and GEMS, one was an illusion and a mystery. Surely I preferred dancing with the love of my life, Budd, but his tune was too offbeat. Budd was a great dancer. However, it wasn't my feet that needed direction; it was my mental rejection that cause me to step off tune.

I recall the first time Budd and I danced, over twenty years ago, in a barracks hallway. Budd's love was like no other. It made my emotions change, like exiting one highway and entering another. It was truly a beautiful relationship. Budd and I had the type of courtship and marriage that our friends envied, but in a good way. I desire my friends to have loving relationships as well, because it minimizes the strain of comparison partner to partner and relationship to relationship.

Budd's love was like an overflow of water—a running reservoir that never pauses for a refill. I had never experienced such a love, nor did I ever want to be without his love. Frankly, I never believed that anything or anyone could ever compare to Budd's love. Also, it was impossible to imagine my trust being reliant upon some untouchable sentiment that was emotional impassive.

It wasn't until later that our career choices of military service would contaminate our relationship with the residue from a war zone, confronting our lives in varying ways and making us vulnerable. It was after about fifteen years of being married to Budd that I learned a more dominant relationship existed. GEMS had become more desired than Budd, who had been my husband for a decade and a half.

GEMS was like a rainbow that made me smile but had the ability to create havoc like a hailstorm. It was a love–hate relationship, but I depended on it. GEMS was the supreme being in my life. It gripped my emotions, refusing to relinquish control. GEMS had the power to change my mood and my thinking; even more so, it made me act as if my every response was a knee-jerk reaction. Can you imagine something controlling your presence to the point that your existence become irrelevant?

My existence seemed dependent upon a power that alienated me, forcing me to be relevant in a way that was obviously irrelevant. It was if I was physically present but mentally absent. I was growing increasingly, day by day, more attached to GEMS. This is who I trusted even more than Budd or myself.

GEMS came into my life at one the most unexpected times ever. I don't believe anyone ever imagines being disassociated from themselves in any context, especially in a mental capacity. I was afraid to acknowledge that this stranger, this ghost, was a part of my corporeal imagery because, after all, a ghost is a corpse without life. Of course, this ghost was alive—living and breathing within my mind, body, and soul.

At times, I thought I was hallucinating, which clearly signified an undetected mental illness. I experienced fantasies, hallucinations, delusions, and alternate reality, causing magnified confusion. I do not believe that most mental illness sufferers will openly admit they are conversing with an unknown life-force, speaking fears into existence by a persuasive power. Subconsciously, I was enthralled with GEMS because it was a listener and confidant, much like my dear friend, Burroni, who showed no judgment regarding my emotional behaviors. This allowed me to fantasize that I was in control even though it was unclear whether I truly digested this divergence.

Now I can admit that it was not me but GEMS that was in control. GEMS and I spent lots of time together once I began complying with the physician's bed rest orders during my medical work leave absence. Often, I would call out to GEMS to appear as if I could touch it. Once upon a time, when I called GEMS and there was no answer, it frightened me, because either I had been abandoned or

I was living a lie. After I had called to GEMS a few more times, it conveyed that, "I was giving you the silent treatment so that your desperate need could sound more animated!" My interaction with GEMS was often like a real-life relationship, where I felt adored and admonished depending upon my actions and responsiveness.

I openly expressed anger, fears, disappointment, and emotion because GEMS dominated my appetite to consume nothing soulfully nourishing but everything spiritually noxious. I shared all this information with my BFF (Benevolent Fairy Forevermore) Burroni, not knowing what her response would be. It was like the sound of a sweet melody, verbally embracing me with the whisper of, "I am here. Just let me be your relief!" It felt like my emotional burdens were lifted by an affection that is hard to explain. Burroni's love is surreal, patient, comical, and yet so sincere.

Before I could say another word, the tears were no longer wet to my skin and flowing down my neck. Burroni listened and responded in a way that gave me hope that I wasn't crazy. Yeah, right, I said it: *crazy*. We chatted for about an hour and then, without hesitation, I got up from the chair and walked out of the closet and into my bedroom. My husband and sons were sitting on the bed and gave a sigh of relief as I exited the closet. I had been sitting in a secluded closet for eight hours, but I acted as if those hours did not exist. I went to the ladies' room; amazingly, as a pregnant woman, I did not have to tee-tee during this extensive jaunt of captivity. It was probably since I'd had nothing to eat or drink.

It was clear to me that this stranger from within wanted to capture me on a more permanent basis. Frankly, I had no clue how to keep GEMS at bay. GEMS was not an innocent bystander but instead an active participant that controlled my emotions, implanting doubt in my ability to act mentally and emotionally stable. GEMS did not ask me questions but rather conveyed its perspective to encourage my actions.

GEMS would routinely, out of thin air, express how unable I was to offer any level of realism to anyone, and assure me that I was just as irrelevant to others. GEMS was convincingly persuasive, but

Burroni and I had a long friendship that I trusted to the mountaintop and back. I knew I had a committed fighter, my BFF, in my corner who would go blow-to-blow with GEMS to save me. Burroni had the endurance to help me break this stranglehold by GEMS so that I could begin to restore my soul and hope to regain my livelihood.

Soon came the sunrise after my two a.m. battle with the foe. My friend and I were exhausted. I was no longer familiar to myself. Something about me had changed. I felt more somber than ever, and my head was pounding. I was overly anxious and depressed about what had happened and what had been revealed. Although I knew that I had never experienced betrayal by GEMS or Burroni, nonetheless, there was still some level of uncertainty.

I asked Budd what he remembered about last night, and he shrugged it off as if it was hormonal and that it was expected for someone pregnant to undergo changing emotions. Budd may have been in denial, much like me. Even he hesitated before gaining more insightfulness as to my health and emotional spiraling. This was an exhale of relief for me, because even though we marry presuming "till death do us part, through sickness and health," no one ever really imagines the ailing detriments of mental illness. Certainly, this may have alarmed my mate, because coping with mental illness requires so much time and energy, not to mention layered medical resources.

Budd stood steadfast throughout my health crisis. From the beginning of our courtship, our souls were rooted with an understanding that not everything is consequential with the exception of marital commitment. Budd and I vowed to ensure our relationship would last no matter the challenge.

My head continued to throb like my brain was searching for an exit door from my chaotic head. I suddenly grabbed my head with both hands, feeling like I would pass out. The ringing in my ears was inconceivably uncomfortable as well; it was like a demon had forced me to depart into another world that was not only painful but eerie. To me, this was the confirmation that I was no longer able to identify with not only my birth name but my very identity. It had become so interconnected with GEMS that it was exported. This was the first time ever that I submissively yet silently admitted that I had submitted to an oppressive power.

I was still me and GEMS was still it, but the it controlled the vulnerable me. This was not a religious conversion, where I etched a new beginning of repentance, but more like a conversion where my mental and physical existence had merged into two minds instead of one. I had become receptive to allowing GEMS to become my spokesperson, which made me more subdued than impulsive, even as a mental duet. Since this was an episode of major concern psychologically, a follow-up medical assessment was initiated with my neurologist. I had repeatedly tried to stifle these feelings but I felt powerless, realizing I was risking the bliss of so many innocent people. Heck, the innocence of myself was alarmingly at risk.

The neurologist once again examined me, conducted several tests, and consulted with me to elaborate regarding my responsiveness to theses painful emotional behaviors. About an hour later, the neurologist summoned me back to the office and presented me with a long piece of paper stating that my bed rest had been extended out of fear for my mental capacity and the threat of an aneurysm and a fourth stroke. This news in and of itself was devastating, but it was critical to me and my unhatched egg. The hospital wanted me under the strictest neurological and obstetric observation.

I was scheduled for admittance into a hospital for a weeklong stay to undergo numerous evaluations. This was tiring, unnerving, and very uncomfortable. I hated hospital stays where I had to remain for long periods. The neurologist wanted to conduct multiple brain scans with an extensive internal assessment of my brain to better understand the sudden changes in my behavior and responsiveness. Five years later, I annually undergo this same brain scan procedure to detect whether any changes have abruptly occurred. Thus far, nothing.

Three days had gone by, and the neurologist notified me that the test had been scheduled for later that night. An experienced technician would come to my room to transport me for a detailed high-tech screening procedure. It was around eight that evening when I heard a knock at my hospital door. A tall Caucasian man entered to verify my name and asked if I was ready to be transported. I obliged but was clearly terrified about the procedure. I had no inclination as to the exact processes involved in such a comprehensive brain procedure.

Once we arrived to the area for the exam, Budd was told he had to sit outside the room and could not accompany me during the procedure. Suddenly, my anxiety was incited as I lay on the examination table. The technician proceeded to prep me for the exam, and then he began to put a football-like apparatus over my head, which caused me to go into compete panic with psychosis. The sound of screaming, kicking, and crying seeped from the doors into the hallway from the exam room. Initially, I did not understand my frightful panic but as seconds passed, it was obvious that it was more than just distress.

The technician was shocked to see this level of claustrophobia, so he stopped the exam. He spoke in a surprised muttering, sharing with serious concerns that, "There is no way this test can be done under these circumstances." He attempted the procedure for a second time after compassionately conveying that the testing was crucial in determining my health complications. Finally, the technician made a call and informed the head neurologist as to what had occurred. The technician then helped me back into the wheelchair and rolled me back to my room escorted by my husband, Budd.

Budd once again could not believe what he was witnessing of my behavior. I could see the confusion in his eyes, like, *What in the hell happened?* This, in my opinion, spurred Budd's realization that something had undeniably changed from within me. My husband was baffled; he appeared disturbed but became anxious to determine what had happened behind those closed doors to make me go from zero to one hundred. Once Budd became aware of my claustrophobic reaction, he reached down to touch my hand. He cuddled my fingers in the palm of his hand as I trundled down the quiet hospital hallway.

The doctors were determined to get this test done, so for the next three days it was a foremost concern to expedite a different medical option to get the procedure completed. The issue was not whether I was available or willing to comply with the procedure but to ensure that specified physicians' schedules were cleared for at least an hour. I needed to be put to sleep and intubated for the procedures, which created life-threatening risks for me and my unborn child. I was about four months pregnant, and the doctors feared that I would go into labor. That fear was apparent in the eyes of the nurse, doctor, neurologist, anesthesiologist, my husband, and of course me.

I felt panicked about being sedated to receive the test in a room filled with such a large medical team. This team of medical personnel understood the risks and had to react immediately once the medication started to take effect. I was mentally deranged, but the nurse tried to inform me of every step of the process. I was in distress: crying, trembling, and holding tightly to my husband as he tried to comfort my fears.

The neurologist heard the nurse's briefing regarding the procedure and beckoned him to the next room. The neurologist scolded the nurse for intensifying the stress levels for all parties involved. I overheard the neurologist telling the nurse that he was not being a professional but instead was creating more paranoia. My husband stood there comforting me until he was informed that it was time to roll me into the room to begin the procedure. My husband was not allowed to witness this process in case something went catastrophically wrong or not as anticipated.

Finally, the medication started to make me dizzy and dazed. Before I realized it, I was unconscious and being rolled by wheelchair into this white-walled room, with numerous people standing over me. I was terrified, but I understood that I had no choice. I was strolled into a black space of darkness much like the one when

GEMS and I were alone. This, however, was a state of pure blackout with prolonged muteness. Per Budd's remembrance, the neurologist came out to notify him that I had been fully intubated and the procedure was underway.

I cannot pinpoint a timeline as to how long I was in the room, but it seemed like hours. I awoke in a recovery room surrounded by nurses, with my husband standing near my bedside. One nurse began asking about my recollection of the procedure and whether I was all right. I felt a bit overwhelmed still, and my throat was very sore from the intubation. I was anxious to know what the neurologist had discovered.

The nurses told me that I could not go home until I had urinated at least five times. They had to ensure that my bladder was emptied of the highly potent medications administered for the procedure. This process took about forty-five minutes. Perhaps frequent urination was easier for me, since pregnancy norms instigate continuous bladder reactions. I was released and told that I would be contacted by telephone when all the results were in so that I could return to the hospital. I was also given various medications to cope with the debilitating migraines and other pains.

My follow-up appointment was a week later. I met with my neurologist and obstetrician and was informed of their concerns. I had not only become a high-risk pregnancy but there was a discussion as to whether to abort the fetus because of my alarming health issues. The medical team's belief was that the child would suffer some type of birth defects. The doctor advised us that his desire was to draw fluid from my embryonic sack, but the procedure was life-threatening to the child.

Budd and I consulted with each other about the anxiety, depression, and who knows what else. Our emotions became heightened as we struggled to make such a difficult decision that could harm our unborn child. My husband looked at me and said, "No. Let's just go through the pregnancy as if it was normal. What will be, will be." He had lots of experience with nurturing disabled children, since his mom was a special education teacher during his adolescent and teen years. Budd's experience assisting his mom with disabled adolescents was emotionally consoling. At this point, I feared I could not do either—abort the child or parent an inactive child. Nevertheless, I was willing to risk not having the test, since Budd's support was so sincere, rational, and heartfelt.

The doctor reentered the room, and we shared that we could not risk the life of this precious egg. We would pray and take our chances. I was told that my appointments would be weekly at this point for cautious monitoring. Also, hospitalization might be necessary, depending upon the progress or regress of my health. I clearly understood that my health was under threat and these ailments had invaded me internally like a venomous demon. I became impacted by something of unknown potency that contributes to voids of comprehension. I was now being forced to face this power without the will to resist.

My husband and I just stared at my belly, wondering how this could be. I still wondered whether the early termination perhaps was the best choice. Nevertheless, I resisted and did not verbalize such a thing. I had come to desire this unborn egg and was hoping it would be the daughter I had prayed for during the past eight years.

I got dressed and gave my husband a hug. We wandered down the hospital hallways before stepping into an empty elevator with mirrors. I laid my swollen hands on my blouse to touch my covered, oily belly and echoed for the first time after realizing the severity of my health, "I love you, my darling baby." I was scared into silence while being scared for the possible demise of my unborn child.

The doctor gave me an appointment to return the following week, which was about five days away. We waited in limbo to discover my health's progress. Each day, I was mesmerized by this little innocent being growing inside me. It would be devastating to uproot this love from the warmth of my nest prior to the nine-month mark. The most anticipated information to us was probably the gender of our unborn child, because it would provide simultaneous closure and commencing.

This upcoming appointment was going to be fateful in comprehending the fate of my health but also the fruition of gender. I am saddened to admit that I could be awarded the fruition of gender and yet be disappointed because of my health, and I could be fortunate to gain a healthy medical report and still be disappointed. It was either a lose–lose situation or a win–win. I did not know what to expect.

Chapter 5

Strangest Rebirthing

It was Monday evening, a day prior to my obstetrician appointment. I reminded everyone that my appointment was scheduled for the following morning at eight o'clock. The anxiety surrounding the health of me and my unborn child was indisputably important. Additionally, we were finally going to find out the gender of the baby—whether a girl or boy.

My eldest son, Parriz, was a senior in high school, but he decided that he would check into school a couple of hours tardy along with my youngest son, Jostein, who was overjoyed to find out whether his dream to be a "big brother" would come true with a little sister or a little brother. He already had an older brother, so he made it clear that he wanted a sister. In fact, we all wanted a girl.

My four-month prolonged meditation with the Almighty was a request to bless us with a healthy princess. I was sleepless the night before the appointment because of the mystery as well as neonatal pounds weighing heavily on my back and mind. I thought that our little bundle of joy must be a girl! Prayerfully, I did not believe that God had put me through all these trials and tribulations to not grant that long-awaited blessing. I am not in any way suggesting that God had to comply with my yearning, but my faith led me to believe that it was my time. Since I had asked, I was ready to receive.

By this time, I was about four months along, and it seemed that

I had a long way to go. I had a rough night and wasn't feeling well. Even so, the joy of confirmation of the unknown gender of my egg made me focus more on good news than bad feelings. We all woke up around six in the morning, and my husband prepared breakfast for me and the boys while we were dressing for the appointment and school. After the appointment, the boys would have to be dropped off at school no matter what the news was.

Of course, the most preferred blessing was to have a healthy baby, no matter the gender, but who am I kidding? Emotionally, we were already facing a dilemma as to whether we should abort the child. This was the last and final time to go forth with the doctor's suggested choice because of my health. We were not considering an abortion at this point, but that could always change based upon the doctor's advice regarding any effects surrounding the condition of either my or the baby's health.

I plainly recall the ultrasound misdiagnosis surrounding the gender during my pregnancy with Jostein, who was born in Germany. We had been told for five months that we were having a girl. The goal was to have a tubal ligation after the birth of my second child, trusting it was a girl, but things did not go as planned. We had decorated the nursery expecting a daughter and were told only one week prior to my delivery date that the gender was not what we had thought. That day, the ultrasound technician asked us specifically, "Do you guys know what you are having?"

My husband and I smiled, and I said, "We sure do. It's a girl!"

The technician replied, "Who told you that? Based upon what I see, it's 100 percent a boy!"

I began to gasp for air as if something had died. I told the technician that he had the test wrong and that we'd had at least four prior ultrasounds depicting features of a girl's genitals. He saw how distraught I was becoming, so he recommended that we return to my personal physician to get clarification. My prenatal care for that pregnancy was provided by a German doctor who had a civilian medical office. We rushed out of the technician's office and went to get confirmation as to what the doctor saw on the monitor versus the ultrasound technician. We were in total shock over the change in gender, but we wanted an answer. We assumed that the technician was wrong. Our optimistic belief was that the German doctor was right, and that it was a girl and not a boy.

We rushed from the office holding hands, empathizing over how to ingest this very unexpected development. Much to our surprise, we saw our maternity physician exiting one of the department stores outside of his office building, and we rushed toward him. He recognized me as one of his patients and asked, "Are you okay?"

I told him, "Absolutely not!"

The doctor asked, "Why?"

I replied, "You told us we were having a girl, and we were just told that we are not—that it's a boy!"

He replied, "You are having a girl. I did the test several times! But let's put your frustrations to rest and conduct another test, without charge, to confirm the earlier test."

We hurried into the exam room before the arrival of his next patient so that he could perform the test. I got undressed, and the doctor performed the test. He turned and look at us both with empathy and disbelief, whispering, "I am so sorry! It is a boy."

I cried and complained, but nothing of course was going to change. Yet I stilled cried. Once we returned from the appointment, I knew my eldest and only child who was a boy was going to take the news hard. Parriz only wanted a sister and not a brother. My assumption was that he feared if it was a boy, it would uproot his preeminence in my life as my firstborn. We were so very close, and I was hoping that would not be the case. A girl would have helped us avoid his perceived displacement as my son. I suppose the firstborn inherently feels entitled in many unspoken ways.

On that long-ago day, we picked Parriz up from school early and decided to choose a place where we could get lunch to lighten the blow of his future brother-hood. We decided to eat at the local Popeye's Restaurant near the Hanau AAFES Exchange, which was an overseas military installation. I proceeded to share with Parriz that we needed to find another name for the baby. He was initially confused but quickly realized what I meant.

The name we had all chosen together as a family was Jalisa. I began to tell Parriz that the doctor had made a mistake, and the baby was a boy instead of a girl. He started screaming and crying in the restaurant. Customers, restaurant workers, and bystanders were staring at us like we had abused our child or something.

I got up and comforted Parriz, whispering near his cheek that everything was going to be fine and that apparently God had a different plan. Soon Parriz stopped sniveling, looked up at me with those beautiful brown eyes, and said, "I guess God wanted me to be a big brother to boy and not a girl."

I said, "You're right, and you're going to be an awesome big brother."

This mistake surrounding gender had occurred over a decade ago, and now this same gender revelation was upon our family once again. We were done eating breakfast, and the hospital drive was about twenty minutes away from our home. I told everyone we better get going because we did not want to be late for one of the best days ever. I was excited and scared all at the same time. A second disappointment would create another stressor for my already volatile pregnancy.

We all got into the car and chatted about little to nothing, which I presumed was due to each of us sheltering our anxieties. Our expressions revealed nothing but nervousness. We arrived at the hospital and were escorted to the exam room. The walk to the building was short in distance, but it seemed long since none of us spoke. We were poker-faced with emptiness, waiting to end our uncertainty.

Once in the exam room, we were greeted by an ultrasound technician who informed us that the doctor would be in shortly. My doctor, Dr. Martinez, was amazing and had become so well-acquainted with us as a provider that she wanted to be included in this process because of the severity of possible complications with the pregnancy. She also wanted to share in the discovery ultrasound news revealing the gender of the baby.

Dr. Martinez knew how badly our family wanted a girl. The procedure began, and we all waited anxiously as different tests were being done in the presence of a room filled with strangers and my family. We all wanted to be surprised, so my family and I were asked to close our eyes for the big reveal. Dr. Martinez completed all the tests, but the monitor was still connected as she cheeringly yelled, "You guys got your wish! It's a girl!"

We all started to yell, reveling with fist bumps as I lay on the table. My husband and sons were so happy. They were finally going to have a daughter and a little sister birthed by me, their wife and mother. This news was so overwhelming that I could have jumped from the table and ran down the halls of the same hospital we had left days earlier with news of distress.

This time, we left the hospital filled with joy and excitement. The kids had to return to school, so we dropped them off as soon as we could and decided to celebrate later that evening with a great dinner. My husband decided to order in Chinese food, which was one of my favorites. However, during this stage of my prenatal period, some foods produced some of the worst gastrointestinal aromas imaginable. I stilled enjoyed it, but I suffered later.

I was so happy about the news that I quickly gathered my nursery-decorating books and began to imagine how beautiful the nursery was going to be. I decided on a fairy-tale theme, with the room's décor filled with different fairies. I believed having a daughter was magical and a dream come true. Just imagine—a little me. We would have a gender connection. I would be priming a princess to someday become a queen.

It's no different from men yearning to have sons. I can relate to men who feel incomplete, and most men I suppose are willing to admit it. They hope for a son to carry on their legacies. I feel a daughter provides the same or an even greater nostalgia, because her capacity to reach humanity is on such a different level. Females inadvertently have a will to nurture other siblings, aging parents, a partner, and eventually their own nest of eggs. There is no doubt that my daughter would change my feeling of relevance as a woman.

Why is that? Just envision in your mind's eye the things your mom taught you, but also the things that she chose not to teach, leaving you room to absorb and nurture your own perspectives. Nothing against my mom's parenting, but there were lots of things that were kept from me because of her inability to openly express what I needed as a woman and not necessarily as a daughter. Womanhood involves different stages of absorption and growth, permitting moms like me to envision who we were and are, and what we hope our daughters will become as we infuse our past with their present. The notion of being accountable to a little girl is incredibly self-indulgent. I vowed wholeheartedly to mold her into the best evolving woman conceivable.

I believe that a woman's relevance is far different from a man's relevance. My desire is that all my children will be relevant in their own chosen capacities, but culturally and socially it has been difficult for women to find their footing. A man's first steps are already ordained as the head. That doesn't mean that all steps are equal, because they are not, but all steps should lead to a passage of appropriate growth.

This long-awaited opportunity to parent a daughter was destined to be great, especially since she was my first daughter. I yearned for a relationship with someone I could support, share deep thoughts with, and teach things that my mom and I did not experience together. My mom was hands-off, with the exception of disciplining me and my siblings. I was tickled pink that I would finally experience a mother-daughter relationship contributing to the evolution of femininity throughout the stages of womanhood. This is an amazing experience, especially when it's your own daughter.

The opportunity to relish the similarities and differences made me wonder whether the view we imagine is truly a reflection of who we appear to be as we age. I made a few missteps in my life that I wish I could relive, even though I know that is impossible. But I could now forewarn my daughter by guiding and advising her so that she might avoid pitfalls that cause unnecessary misery and disappointment. Appreciation of my misadventures would hopefully privilege me to clear some barriers from her passage, minimizing unnecessary mileage on her mind and soul. Everyone undergoes trials and triumphs involving transformational changes; however, not every step of growth is progressive. Sometimes, regression proffers lessons that help to bridge future gaps.

It was finally time to meet this amazing egg that I was anxious to birth after nine long months of medical complications. I would now have to spend more time nurturing a newborn instead of daily routines of conversing with GEMS. Throughout my pregnancy, my health was erratically unstable, inducing anxiety and uncertainty on a multitude of levels—mental, emotional, hormonal, psychological. I was hopeful that if hormonal, these anxieties would quickly vanish so my fairy-tale tea parties could begin with my princess.

GEMS and I had been closet partners for almost five months throughout my pregnancy, but I prayed the relationship's end would coincide with my gestational delivery. Budd and I knew the exact day that we would have our bundle of joy in our loving arms. Previously, we had asked the doctor to medically induce me if my little one was resisting her runway slide into the world on her expected due date. Additionally, Budd had an overseas job awaiting his arrival that had already been postponed for two weeks.

The morning I was supposed to be labor-induced, I felt discomfort in my pelvic region and in my mind. Suddenly, I felt dread and fear over the pain surrounding childbirth. It was a pain I was all too familiar with, having given birth twice before.

Months earlier, the doctor had discussed the possibility of an epidural as a cautionary yet preventive measure to avoid any cerebral dangers, since I was a high-risk pregnancy case. The doctor reiterated that this was a necessary precaution after careful review of my medical history. I had suffered three previous ministrokes (TIAs) as well diagnoses of mental lapses throughout the pregnancy. Of course, this unpredictable reminder regarding my health intensified my birth anxiety to deliver this precious egg.

I am certain this resilient egg was just as ready as I to be rescued from the darkness. I had suffered through the agonies of uncertainty with only one thing being for certain: at last, a daughter! I had imagined in my heart who she would look like, her skin tone, her eyes, her hair, and so on. However, no matter who or which sibling she resembled, it would be like cuddling a pot of gold, for this was truly a golden blessing.

The night before my delivery, I felt even more restless than ever before, filled with joy and impatience to hold my princess for the very first time. Childbirth is most surely one of the purest forms of unconditional love and pain, bonded together by birthing a life and coalescing into one of the most profound emotions ever. The pain is temporary, but the love is everlasting, beyond a lifetime that surpasses Earth, etching an eternity of connection far into the heavens above.

Late that night, as everyone slept, GEMS beckoned me to the closet. I was restless, so I obliged, entering our pitch-black meeting place with instructions to GEMS to keep our voices muffled to avoid awakening Budd. I did not want to alarm him about this secret love affair with GEMS, but it was fulfilling to chat with GEMS and ease my mind about the discharge of childbirth. GEMs wanted to converse with me about the experience of childbirth and the relevance GEMS and this baby would have in my life. I was upset with GEMS, because GEMS was becoming egotistically arrogant, expressing superiority to everything and everyone, to include even me. I reminded GEMS that even though I needed the support, I had prayed for years for a daughter, and I would not let GEMS come between us.

GEMS became inflamed with anger, screaming at me, "We will see about that! No one comes before me!"

I was shocked by both GEMS's tone and message. I was unable to respond to GEMS because, as I opened my mouth to do so, it felt as though it was inadvertently sealed. No words could escape from my lips. It didn't matter, because GEMS had vanished from the closet. I returned to my bed with only a couple of hours before it was time to rise.

Chapter 6

An Egg-Stranger Is Untied

The morning had arrived when the physician would perform the labor inducement so that I could delivery this mysterious egg from within my womb. It was about five thirty in the morning, before sunrise, and I turned to Budd muttering, "Today is the day that I get to meet *me* in an altered soul!"

He grinned and asked, "Are you ready?" He also asked whether I was afraid.

I replied, "Yes, Babe, but I do not believe I will be labor induced. My back is aching like never in the past." It felt like this mystery egg was ready to reveal itself without any facilitation from the doctor.

This moment was becoming more magical than I had dreamed. From this day forward, I would at last have a daughter. Budd and I shared a love that ran beneath the depth of our souls. No matter our past or present, we were excited about the future of our family with this new addition.

I arose slowly from the bed, grabbed my robe, and walked into the beautiful, barren nursery to gaze at its eye-catching splendors. The most vivid was the lavishly cream-decorated bed that would comfort my egg for days, months, and years to come. This room was one of comfort, enabling me to tour a mommy-land with mesmerizing lullabies that ensconced my mind with unimaginable contentment, even though I rarely sang. Spellbinding melodies of the new life that God had entrusted me with as the mother-hen filled my mind. Budd snapped several photos of me in the nursery, since I wanted to evoke the austere infant's room and then rejoice in her arrival with a sanctified prayer after her birth. Additionally, I wanted to share this joyous escapade with my mom, who had never witnessed the birth of either of my children, although she had with my other siblings.

After this emotional overload of thinking too far ahead, even if only days, I had to revert to present-day life, because one never fully knows God's plan. Filled with anticipation and enthusiasm, I got dressed and ate small amounts of breakfast to avoid any surprising misadventures during delivery, as had occurred with my earlier pregnancies—what an embarrassment! After gathering all my things for the hospital, I called my two boys to the family room and let them know that today would be the day. It was time to exalt. The boys would have a sister today, March 21, by the end of school.

I arrived at a newly built civilian hospital located in the city of El Paso. The staff and physicians were amazing the entire time I received treatment—with the exception of one occasion, which I may describe later. I arrived at the hospital and reported to the area where my labor inducement was planned for egg deliverance; however, that plan changed shortly after my arrival. The labor and delivery nurse examined me and revealed that I was already in labor and measured at two centimeters. I was happy but nervous because of my medical condition.

The staff worked quickly and seemed relieved that they did not have to force the egg by inducement because of a possible rebellious passage into the world. Instead, my courageous egg was ready to journey into a world of light far different from her past nine months of darkness. Hold on! I imagine the egg felt rushed, because dilation stopped. I guess she wanted to walk the runway at her own pace!

The nurse sighed with relief. This would give the doctor time to deliberate as to whether the prior decision to administer an epidural would be best for my health. Shortly thereafter, the doctor once again confirmed the gender of our egg and then examined me. She agreed to proceed with the epidural, since other complications were coming into play.

You know that scary anxiety called blood pressure? My blood pressure was somewhat low, and the goal was to avoid any other medical crisis. Thus, I received an unusual dosage for the epidural, which made me numb as nails. I had no feeling anywhere below my breasts. I couldn't even lift my legs; they felt like hundred-pound sandbags. It was amazing that my body could be molten on top and frozen below. My body reminded me of this amazing hot and cold tea that I drank at one of my favorite Chinese restaurants while living in Germany. The top of the tea was sweet and cold, and the bottom was hot and tangy. Mmm, so delicious!

The time was quickly approaching, confirming the doctor's timeline that had been previously projected. Yes, delivery was near. I was fully dilated and ready to deliver the golden egg. The delivery would take place between seven thirty and eight that evening, after sunset. This would be perfect, because it would give my two boys time to get out of school, grab something to eat, and return to the hospital as sibling bystanders to witness the birth of their sister. Well, not exactly witnesses at my bedside, but in the nearby waiting area, which was only about twenty feet from my delivery room. Can you imagine your two sons eye-witnessing the birth of a sibling? That would have been too graphic of a shock wave, revealing a birthing of life while compromising the future of my maternal privacy.

The boys arrived at the hospital around six thirty that evening and seemed excited as well uneasy as to what to expect. I too was nervous but also excited, knowing today I would enrich my life by sealing my birthing fate to nest a daughter. It was awkward, because even though I previously mentioned that my sons could not witness my egg-hatching, I almost changed my mind to endorse their request. Good-naturedly and calmly, Budd looked at all three of us and groaned. "That's not a good idea," he said. "There's a waiting room right outside the doorway, and the boys should wait there and watch television." Budd promised to rush and get them as soon as the baby made her way onto the stage of life. The doctor permitted us to have one last conversation, with anticipation pending for the big moment. Dr. Martinez would return in approximately fifteen minutes to prep me for the deliverance of this precious golden offspring.

Suddenly, the time had arrived, and my hospital room was filled with medical professionals, include a neurologist to monitor my neurological state and respond with haste if anything traumatic occurred. I was serene, because I felt absolutely no pain whatsoever while preparing to give birth. I must admit, an epidural is the best birth pain relief on the market for expectant mothers. All I could think of was, *Where in the hell was that epidural during my first two births? Why wasn't I informed as to the power an epidural had to ease the slightest pain or discomfort?* I laughed when the doctor began examining me for the ultimate finale, the initial push. I thought, *This is insane. I do not feel a thing waist-down. That's what you call pain-free!*

The professionals all assumed their delivery positions, and the doctor mumbled that since I had a torrential dosage of epidural, she would have to tell me when to push because I had no pain to give me a cue. This is one of those instances when the phrase "No pain, no gain" is absolutely untrue.

There were monitors attached in different places, but all I could think of was getting started so I could say goodbye to this large belly blocking my view of the doctor. I yearned to greet this mysterious egg that I wanted to see, hold, kiss, and introduce myself to for the very first time. My husband grabbed the camcorder to videotape this blissful occasion. Customarily, it would have been gauche because of the enduring pain and stressfulness that would undoubtedly require him to be at my bedside comforting me. This time, however, it was not needed. He was just as amazed as I was.

The doctor told me, "Push!"

I pushed and grunted softly.

The doctor said to hold for a minute and wait until she told me to push again. I was even more anxious, listening unwearyingly for the next command.

"Push now!' a voice screeched. "She's coming! Push!"

Out popped my golden egg. I heard my husband say, "Hi, Landowyn." He teared up and whispered, "She's so beautiful."

I could not wait to see her. Everyone surrounding my bedside was echoing the same sentiments as to her beauty.

We had decided on her name over five months before her birth. I wanted to incorporate my maiden name to reflect her Indian heritage, so the name was chosen like so. Her name was so special because it was mostly my maiden name with the letter *y* inserted at the end of it.

Landowyn was almost eight pounds and nearly thirty inches long. She had beautiful golden skin tone with blue eyes and plump pink lips. She looked like a real-life doll that moved slowly and whimpered with a discreet cry. I could not believe the golden egg was glistening in golden tones. Her skin reflected such a canvas that circulated nothing but multidimensional hope and happiness for our family.

The doctor brought her to me so that I could get a glimpse of her. I was breathless to look at this paragon of purity, filled with nothing but innocence. Oh my God! Her gracious being filled my heart. It had been over eight years of praying for such a miracle. Thank you, Almighty God, for such a blessing. My gratitude overflowed. I couldn't wait to share her with the boys, so I asked Budd to go get them, and he hurried out of the room.

Landowyn was clothed and carried over to the incubator to finish her cleanup, purging her of womb debris acquired during her travels. As they continued to clean her and perform vitals, the door opened, and the boys entered my room. The nurse walked toward my bed and positioned Landowyn in my arms. It was the exclamation point to my existence, filling a void so heartfelt that I never felt so wholesome. The boys embraced the moment and stared in disbelief that she was finally here. We no longer had to imagine her manifestation but could see her materialization in real life.

They touched and chattered words to their little sister, and they seemingly felt as complete as I did, especially our youngest son. My eldest son, Parriz, was surprisingly a bit shy about it. I suppose he felt another sibling had taken his place in my life, not realizing that I had enough space and love for all three. Even to this very day, I do not believe he feels as interconnected as I had hoped and prayed he would.

I stayed in the delivery room for about an hour and talked with my family while sharing our joyful thoughts. The boys did not want to leave but had to return home to prepare for school the next day. My stay in the hospital lasted about two more days. I rested and became more acquainted with my daughter. This was a renewing process, learning to care for an infant once again, but I was ready to oblige. After all, it had been a decade since I had held a baby of my own—one who would be dependent upon me for everything.

Normally, I would have had help with the routine of tending to a baby, but my darling Budd had taken a job in Afghanistan as a contractor. Unfortunately, jobs stateside for veterans seemed impossible to secure, even though companies proclaimed to be hiring talent-skilled veterans. This has been a sore spot in our lives— that so many veterans struggle to gain employment after they have risked their lives. Few organizations honor their implied obligation. Veterans deserve to be employed so that they can return to normal life with civility. Since Budd was a man of principle determined to provide for our family, he without hesitation left for his overseas employment a mere seven days after the birth of our daughter. This seemed unfair and certainly undeserved for Budd, as he would miss so much of her infancy.

Budd loved his family so much, and he understood his obligation to us as the breadwinner. No one in my family could financially afford to visit and help during this time of need. Neither did I want to further extend myself financially. I had become financially exhausted as a constant giver with little or no return.

Moms wear so many different hats, requiring diversified functioning as a productive parent. This was just one more fashion head accessory, although this hat demanded priority wear. I still had a military career as a logistics officer that was totally demanding of my time. Fortunately, I had almost three months to contemplate my added responsibilities during my authorized maternity and vacation leave that was granted per my request.

The day for Budd to leave us drew near. He would be away for the next four months. We intentionally sidestepped each other throughout the day, hoping to avoid the emotional downturn it would inflict, even though we had agreed on this opportunity during my pregnancy. My distress over the fact that my spouse was leaving left me incapable of satisfying him intimately. Four long months, and the level of intimacy that we desired to share was inconceivable because of my giving birth, adhering to the six-week rule, and overwhelming stress from a new infant that I dared not complain about.

The departure was hard on Budd and the boys, but not our dear Landowyn. She, of course, had not a worry in the world. Our princess had no way of knowing that her father's breath would not kiss her soft, golden skin for the next several months. I noticed the gentleness in the way he held her throughout the day, especially during each feeding. Budd pretty much cared for her the entire day. The day prior, Budd, Landowyn, and I went to take our princess's first professional portrait so that our family could cherish having a picture with her and her dad. Returning to us from a combat zone was not guaranteed, and he could not be assured he would hold her another time. Capturing such a moment was momentous for us both.

Later that night, I printed the lavender and baby blue photo and inscribed it with the words, "My Father, My Friend, My First Love," gifting him with one of the most precious connections between a dad and a daughter. I could see the tears glistening on his red-tone skin as he smiled with pride.

This was a major sacrifice. However, we were prepared as military professionals. Selflessness was an expected trait of character, even it was absent prior to military service. It was a definite compromise, but with great potential regarding our future stability. I preferred the sacrifice now rather than later for our family, especially since military retirement was approaching.

Budd's trip to Afghanistan was scheduled to begin with a late-night flight from El Paso. Budd decided this flight choice would make it emotionally easier on everyone, so he booked a cab to the airport. As a wife, I felt it was odd to say our goodbyes from home while he waited at an airport that was only eight minutes away. Nevertheless, we kissed, hugged, and said our goodbyes. We all teared up, but I believe our youngest son cried the most.

This was not Budd's first job in Afghanistan, it was his second, which led me to believe that I could handle the bills, family duties, chores, new baby, and of course, my own career. Women oftentimes have so much on our plates, so I saw this as another pea in the pod. As moms, we hardly ever second-guess our duties or stress about who is going to take care of us after we take care of everyone and everything. This has become a femininity fiasco that women neglect to address as wives, mothers, and careerists. We must recognize that we need help and are incapable of being Superwoman. We need to be cured of the susceptibility to multitasking that is a detriment to a woman's stability. It is not only self-induced but also a generational expectation.

The baby was only about seven days old, and I had fooled myself into believing that I was a phenomenal woman who cooks, cleans, cares for the children, and has a successful career. All these Cs led to blindness, preventing sight of a literal reality.

About three days after Budd left, Burroni called to share that she was coming to visit and meet her godchild. Burroni was so thrilled to be a godmom. She had planned to stay for about ten days, and I was just as eager about her visit.

During my pregnancy, Burroni would have boxes and boxes delivered to my house for the baby, and she shared my taste in purchasing and gifting etiquette. We were so much alike; we even shared the same birthday, the fifth of February. I bet few besties share that one-of-a-kind datum. However great it is to share the same birthday, I sometimes gift her late. On the other hand, Burroni is never late gifting me or my children, no matter what the milestone is—birthday, graduation, holiday, anniversary, or just thinking of you. What an amazing friend!

She is that ride-or-die friend who was my personal interventionist when I desperately needed closet therapy. We had a lot to catch up on in addition to enjoying the birth of my daughter and Burroni's new role as godmother. She arrived for her visit a month after my delivery. Her flight arrived around noon, so Landowyn and I left for the airport around eleven thirty, since it was only minutes from my house. We waited for her at the baggage claim area.

Moments later, I heard that Italian accent cry out, "Hey, Sunshine!" She was giggling and smiling as bright as the name that she had given me over seven years earlier. She rushed over to me as I cuddled the baby in my arms, wrapping both of us in a humongous hug and kissing us on the cheek. Next, she grabbed the baby from my arms and just laughed, and she spent all the way home in the car in a tête-à-tête of baby chatter. I pulled her luggage as she carried the baby so they could continue their social connection, which was amazingly affectionate. She cherished this little bundle of joy just as I did. I felt blessed to have a friend so genuine.

During Burroni's visit, she was absolutely all-hands-on-deck. Her being there permitted me to catch up on sleep, rest, and recover, but also to enjoy being a new mom. She helped to care for the baby in so many ways, often keeping her goddaughter in the room with her during the night. I can imagine most new moms might not feel comfortable with this level of closeness, but I absolutely was smitten. The unconditional love she had for me as a friend had now poured over onto my daughter.

Burroni and I are so much alike; even my kids are flabbergasted. These similarities carried over into my daily routines regarding other chores. Burroni cleaned, cooked, ironed, shopped for groceries, and did laundry. She even ran my dog, Deuce, each morning during her visit. Now tell me, what kind of friend does all this and then some?

My treasured friend, Burroni, comprehended the gravity of her advocacy when most needed and wanted. I do not believe a family member could have rendered the level of kindness that she extended with a cheerful smile. I believe Burroni understood that something emotionally was different about me. Nevertheless, she withheld her speculations until I was explicitly ready to grant her inclusive ingress into the mysteries of my health. The idea of full disclosure brought panic, for some things were purposefully exclusive to only me and GEMS.

At first, my meetings with GEMS were disclosed to no one. GEMS stayed coupled only to me and would vanish or shush its voice if there were bystanders. Even if I expressed the existence of GEMS to Burroni, I did not fear that Burroni would shun me or no longer desire to be my BFF. I instead feared being exposed in a way that I might perhaps be irresponsive to questions for which I had no answer. I suppose Burroni understood, because she did not pry for a response. She simply allowed me to be lost, knowing confidently that I would find myself somehow and someday.

A friend who allowed me to tread through my emotions was exactly what I needed. Oftentimes, it is not advice we seek but a listening ear to give solace to our fears. It's odd how you can trust a friend more than you can trust family. Preferring friend over family has taught me that not all blood is thicker than water, for it has become diluted by disparaging inferences that destroy trust.

Finally the time came when Burroni had to return to her military duties in North Carolina. She was one of the most extraordinary soldiers I knew, as reflected in her work ethic, morality, service to others, and fearlessness. I prepared to take Burroni back to the airport after she hugged and kissed the boys goodbye. Afterward, she and our bundle of joy loaded themselves into the car along with her overstuffed luggage. We laughed and joked on the short drive, but my heart was weeping. Although I needed her to stay, I could not verbalize the desperation of my need. She had given me and my children so much that I had to resist my urge to even hint at such of a request. I was trying to ignore the frantic pleas to surrender to the metaphoric stranger, GEMS.

GEMS haunted me day in and day out, aiming to control my mind-set by impeding my recovery with relentless attacks to destroy any lingering human relationships. GEMS would appear out of thin air to make me second-guess any decisions I made. On one occasion while Burroni was visiting, GEMS aimed to make me distrust her.

I mentioned earlier that the baby would sometimes spend the night in Burroni's room so I would not have to get up throughout the night. I agreed because I needed the rest, and it would allow them bonding time. In fact, I wanted Burroni to enjoy the closeness of motherhood; she had no children of her own. I was tickled pink that she yearned for infant intimacy.

Later that night, after we had departed to our bedrooms, I lay comfortably in my bedroom enjoying the silence of not even the slightest melody from the barren bassinette. Unexpectedly, GEMS whispered, "Wake up! Wake up! That devil is going to smother the little one!"

I replied, "GEMS, what are you talking about?"

"You shouldn't ever leave strangers with the baby. Who knows what they are capable of?"

I was speechless, but did not want to negate GEMS's fear of my BFF, Burroni. Certainly, I did not want to believe this admonition, but neither did I want to ignore it. I quickly jumped from the bed and rushed into the room where Burroni and Landowyn lay with heavenly smiles upon their faces. I tiptoed over to Landowyn's crib, snatched her quickly, and cuddled her away in my timid arms as I whisked us both back to my bedroom.

GEMS had planted distrust of anyone in my mind, making it difficult to listen to anyone with sincerity unless GEMS did not interject a different perspective. Burroni never knew what really inspired me to retrieve bundle of joy that night. She never asked, so I never revealed the cause and effect of my decision.

I never tried to keep GEMS away, but I did not ask for it with any summons. It was like a friend who needs or requires my presence, just like my BFF, Burroni, who was set to depart to board her flight. I gave Burroni a big hug and thanked her for breathing life into my world. She turned, looked at me, and said, "I am only a call away. Do not hesitate to call me for anything. I'll be on the first flight."

Burroni beckoned me to release Landowyn from my arms. She held the bundle of joy tightly with such tender arms, whispering how much she loved this child and that she would always be there for her. Any children who have godparents who love them like their own are truly blessed.

Off went Burroni down the airport tunnel toward security, waving and smiling. I returned home and begin to conduct my daily nothing-to-dos. I still had about two weeks before returning to work. My present struggle was to keep GEMS at bay to avoid any mental cruising of my thoughts and emotions.

I knew a confrontation between me and the foe was inevitable. GEMS was a confidante at the beginning of my mental illness, but in later years I began to comprehend that it was purposely seeking to destroy me in an overt strategy with covert intentions. Clearly, it was not acting in my best interest. GEMS had inflicted a multitude of issues: urging me to commit suicide and homicide; daring me to check into a mental hospital; inciting distrust among those I loved; urging me to abort my unborn fetus; animating me to lash out in rage unreasonably; emboldening me to assault two family members; and encouraging me to reject my own existence. GEMS was no doubt powerful! It was obvious that eventually I would have to face this stranger from within if I were to ever regain a healthy and prosperous life with limitless possibilities.

I'd had a bountiful life before GEMS. If I surrendered without a fight, it meant that I had succumbed to a demonic spirit, and that would prove to be my greatest defeat. This trial of tribulations was no quiz but unquestionably one of the most challenging tests ever administered without notes, preparations, or instructions. It seemed as if I was the only scholar with a tutor of cruel intentions waiting to luxuriate in my failure.

It was like a complex multiple-choice quiz where the answers were similar yet so different. There, buried in the responses, was the awkward simplicity of a one-word catchphrase, much like the therapies of mental illness treatments. There is not one specific or same treatment for all mental illness sufferers. It must mirror the psyche of that one person.

The dark room GEMS and I often frequented had imprisoned my mental consciousness, causing an emotional unconsciousness. This infestation of uncertainty had literally imploded in me one of the most crucial organs known to humanity: the brain.

Chapter 7

GEMS, the Stranger, Gains a Foothold

My house became an expanded closet of darkness, segregating multiple rooms behind walls—not only just that hidden-away space in my bedroom. I had nowhere to run because of the relentless power of this stranger who had the freedom to harass me at will. There was very little to occupy my time once the boys had left for school, the baby was quietly asleep, and my husband was still away in Afghanistan.

With very few visitors, if any, knocking at my door to check on me, my ship began to go off course. I had become an antisocial butterfly morphed back into a careless caterpillar waiting to rebirth inside out. This stagnancy of my being allowed GEMS to gain strength from within my state of mind, depressing my effort to resist and fight the foe.

GEMS was not intentionally harmful but rather inadvertently, woundingly cruel. My imbalanced consciousness became a double-minded downfall, encountering a more penetrable counterattack to defend against because of the persistency of this antagonistic yet influential supremacy of control. I did not know which mind was thinking. Was it my mind or was it GEMS's mind? However, one thing I do recall is that they both were intensely in a state of unbearable opposition, causing me to feel imprisoned by a lack of comprehension. GEMS was aggressive, while my shifting efforts seemed only a bit assertive in my responses to fight back.

The truth of the matter is, GEMS was a safe haven, and I liked or maybe even loved having GEMS present as my beloved confidant. GEMS's presence was always embedded in the back of my mind but also at the forefront of my thinking. My capacity to think and rationalize basic things was challenged. Somehow, GEMS provided stable reassurance to get through difficult moments as I tried to articulate my thoughts and the things I needed to do.

I would often walk away so that I could be alone with GEMS to divulge my thoughts audibly. GEMS and I could graciously deliberate my concerns from time to time. It was soothing to know that at the beckoning of my tongue, a nonjudgmental advocate would agree or offer advice that I so desired, even if it was bad. GEMS's companionship was becoming so frantically craved that I valued it more than I valued myself. However, this is not something I would ever admit to anyone. It seemed the tables had turned on me. Instead of GEMS stalking my emotions, the reverse was that I was now stalking GEMS for empathy. I desired responsiveness to confirm my self-identity, which was slowly drowning, with the likelihood that I could become an imperiled species of humanity.

I felt powerful knowing that I had two brains instead of one. There was no way I could not overcome anything, let alone succumb to a MH issue. So I continued my cerebral toasts to GEMS because it was a nod to my secrecy to be buried away in darkness where no sunlight could enter. Our relationship became stronger and stronger, much like a marriage, with a commitment deeper than the ocean and higher than any mountaintop. This was not only a love affair with a stranger but a connubial connection that had powers beyond the land I lived in.

Although I recognized that GEMS had begun to control my actions, reactions, and emotions in an unusual way, I yet continued this craze-fulfilling escapade. I had become powerless and ill without realizing that my condition was due to unknown ailments that I disregarded. The unraveling of my mind and spirit were evidently approaching a breakdown that was only steps around the corner. The only problem was, I had no inclination as to who, what, why, where, and when this emotional strangeness had entered my life, nor the causes beckoning it to come forward into my life.

Now that I reflect on it, was it life's stressors, traumatic incident overload, heredity, or a scientific behavioral response to a medical condition? The origination of mental illness can be unpredictable and without warning. I am not sure of how a health crisis can arise, nor can I presume to answer why someone else may suffer or struggle with mental illness as I have. This is my own unique experience.

Mental illness is a mind-altering disorder that, even after you acknowledge the effects, may yet be unclear as well as uncertain. The blurriness stemming from my uncertainties arose on a day when I was mostly happy-go-lucky at the onset of a morning that changed, all of a sudden, to a gloomy, sad afternoon. I was completing a few chores and decided to feed my daughter before taking my daily ritual of soaking in a hot bath. I had no idea that I was emotionally spiraling, like a fallen bird from the blue skies with injured wings, lacking the control to stop. I needed a moment to try to gain quiet serenity, so I decided the baby would be better off if I put her down.

I placed my daughter in a crib that I had in my bedroom, located at the footboard of my bed. My husband was not comfortable with Landowyn sleeping in her nursery, even though it was the room next to ours. Budd feared the room's location and security from intrusion, since it was located near the front door on a regularly traveled street. I obliged him in his decision and comforted her each night in our lonesome room minus Budd's presence. Landowyn rarely occupied her nursery unless it was for infant play, Pamper changing, or bathing time. I kept her within proximity to me so I could grasp the gravity of this miracle as well as cuddle her regularly.

Landowyn is often referred as my golden egg that laid deep in the crevice of my warm womb. I sometimes call her Goldwyn. When you love someone so deeply, it is sometimes difficult to refrain from only one reverential context when they mean so many more adorations.

As I continued to caress my little love and joy, she fell asleep after a warm bottle and a tuneful lullaby of "You Are My Sunshine." She always beamed to the tune as if it tickled her insides. I quickly lay her in the cushioning of her musical bassinet, anticipating she would sleep as sweetly as the cuddling song.

I rushed to fill the bath so that I could get some relaxation before preparing dinner for the boys, who would be home in three or four hours. I had drawn my bubbly bath and closed the door into the bedroom nearly shut to keep any noise from awakening my little princess. As I proceeded to get into the tub, I was not feeling all that well—still in kind of a somber mood. After sitting in the tub, I started to reflect on how my life seemed barren and my futuristic expectations regarding my life would never be of any measurable value.

I cannot exactly pinpoint my mood. My only recollection is that being present but absent from my own realities and relevancy left me feeling shut out. There really was no one close to whom I could convey my concerns or fears over how my life was changing in a way that I assumed to be regressive instead of progressive. My career had changed, my goals were unclear, and I regularly felt deserted because of my spouse's absence, family discord, and callous leaders of my profession.

I often wonder if, had Budd been physically accessible versus on telephone standby, things would have been different, especially my dependence upon GEMS, of which I had become so fond and loving. My emotions suddenly took over, as though there were no options or choices to relieve me of my distorted thinking. It was if words of nuisance were swirling in the air like a whirlwind, making me feel depleted. Some of the words were: "You are worthless, a failure, and all alone!" The fact of the matter was that it all seemed true at that time and in that setting. My emotional net worth was null and void, because my existence seemingly yielded no measurable profit for me or my family. There was no one to confirm my worth to them, which left me feeling bankrupted.

Teary, with wet swollen eyes, and feeling worthless, I needed a way out of this misery. Abruptly, GEMS entered the room and entwined my contemplations with counsel that I did not request. GEMS felt superlatively unchallenged and did not have a care about interrupting my sacred train of thought. GEMS's voice waved back and forth over the waters in the tub.

Initially, GEMS's visits were never without comfort, whether I needed a laugh or to vent an emotion. This time seemed different. GEMS only wanted to advise and not acknowledge any of my anxieties, even though they were apparent on my distraught canvas. My emotions were hard to hide; I wore them on my sleeve.

GEMS intruded into my silence, as if providing a way to rid me of my melancholy distress. This was the first time I clearly heard my birth name called as the voice muttered softly, "Susie, you are better off being gone and all by yourself! You don't have to put up with being ignored and deserted by those who claim to love and support you. You can show them, and I know just how to make them pay."

My eyes and ears were wide open, and I was emotionally pacified by this suggestive attempt to deplete myself with utter numbness. The question was, how did I become so disconnected to even consider such a thing? I had become submissive to anything that GEMS muttered, even if it conflicted with who I aimed to be, or at least who I thought I was.

Before questioning GEMS's suggestion, I started to slide deeper and deeper into a tub filled to its rim. Without my conscious intention, the waters were lugging me slowly and purposefully toward a boundless abyss where I would have no ability to intervene against this mysterious force. I was taking orders from this sequestered stranger, GEMS, who I had become acquainted with as a source of dark, grave-like solace. Oh my, a demonic spirit intended a watery grave of sorrow for me!

In the past and even now, I was so afraid of being under water, so this is without question an example of how powerful GEMS had become. I had superficially surrendered my will to live. By now, the lukewarm water covered my entire body. Only the tip of my nose was peaking out from the flood. My eyesight, hearing, and soul were drowning beneath the high waters. I sank deeper and deeper, becoming emotionally drowned by all my worldly surroundings.

I was unaware as to what was taking place. It felt like I was buried alive and disabled with no apparent external injury. There were certainly injuries that could not be seen on the surface of my body. However, these wounds were deeply tucked away beneath hidden layers of skin. GEMS was suppressing my ability to defend myself from domination. I was about to be seduced to death by a stranger, a foe, a friend. But then, a more powerful spirit entered.

Unexpectedly, a loud scream came from the room, as though someone was crying for help. It was my defenseless and dependent daughter, Landowyn, crying out for my attentiveness. The irony of it all is that I was the one crying out for attention, but silently. My cry for help was spiritually transcended to my baby by some higher power to awaken me and salvage my soul.

In my mind, I was rescuing my crying infant, but in fact I was the one being rescued. I soared from the tub with water spilling over. Streams of droplets soaked the floor, sabotaging the bathroom's wood, as well the entryway into the carpeted bedroom. I rushed over to the crib and grabbed my screaming child, wondering at the cause of her cries. As soon as I cuddled her in my arms, she hushed as if nothing was wrong. I was perplexed for a moment, and then I returned her to the crib, winding the music mobile to soothe the death-filled atmosphere of ghastly stress.

I returned to the water-soaked bathroom to look at myself in the mirror. I was drenched from head to toe. I looked as if I had been baptized and given a second chance at life to figure out what was going on. I was emotionally stunned and trying to comprehend what had led to this almost tragic event. GEMS had consumed me, causing a lapse in considering the impact to my family, especially my children.

I began to weep, thinking about the boys coming home to find my body lifeless in a tub. What would that have done to them? What would they have thought of me as their mother? It was unthinkable, and it compelled me to relive the moments leading up this watershed that nearly led to the suffocation of my life.

Days went by. I felt total disgust with myself. I still did not know where to turn for help. I could not dare talk of this incident with my husband, who was still employed in Afghanistan, building a better financial portfolio for our family. This incident made chills run up and down my spine. Was I suicidal? Was it post-partum depression? Or was it perhaps the beginning of a bigger issue? No doctor had ever diagnosed me with post-partum symptomatically. Presumably, this encounter between my consciousness and unconsciousness was not nearly over. It was only the beginning.

A few more days passed, and I was feeling afraid and alone. I grabbed a notebook and preceded to write down my emotions to better understand what was going on, but I was too fidgety. Unable to express what I was feeling, I decided to scribble words onto the paper that depicted how I felt. The first word that I recall scribbling on the paper was *numb*. I felt disoriented in my own life and cold toward other people, like I had disassociated from the people around me. This included my children. Even though I interacted with them daily on a physical level, I offered minimal nurturing or affection toward them.

I felt guilty in a myriad of ways, ranging from my lack of involvement as a parent to my pretense surrounding the deflection of my illness. The deception was not toward others but instead to myself. It is impossible to admit something to someone else before acknowledging it to yourself. I was pretending to be fine, but I was panicking with regret and remorse, afraid expose the symptoms of an uncertain illness.

This experience was so out of this world. My psyche had escaped to a different place as I stood in the same place with the same surroundings. I clearly had expanded my emotive self too sporadically without any gravity to ground me psychologically. This incident unquestionably substantiated that I was losing my emotional battle and the tumultuous stranger, GEMS, was prevailing in its demonic dominance.

A few weeks later, I recall traveling about an area in El Paso that I frequented often. At this point, I had lived in El Paso for almost five years, and I knew the different routes like the back of my hand—especially those in proximity to my home. The route that I was traveling usually took about fifteen minutes to drive from point A to point B. This time, it took about two hours. I could not figure out how to navigate my way as I had previously done so many times.

I was in the car with my infant daughter and youngest son, Jostein, who asked, "Are we lost? Why do we keep circling past our house? We could have stopped a while ago," he stated. I was stunned and shocked that he was so observant and knew how to get home, but even more traumatized by my inability to get home from anywhere.

I sniveled silently, and for the first time I recognized that I could no longer hide my condition from anyone, not even my ten-year-old son. My mental lapse had been revealed right before my eyes, but it wasn't what I wanted to see or was willing to see. Once more, I brushed it off as a coincidental misfortune or perhaps being overwhelmed by life's demands.

Why is it that people struggle with adversities that disable some but enable others with engagement to defeat? Everyone experiences something that demands they stop and notice and then react and move forward, whether it's being in love or suffering from the loss of something or someone. The capacity to acknowledge inconsistency in your life shows courageous maturity to confront whatever it may be. However, I had become a coward, fearful of what GEMS would do or think of me. At the same time, I was thoughtless in contemplating what those who mattered—my minor children— thought or noticed about my strange behaviors.

Jostein noticed, but he did not express himself during our precarious journey home. Later that evening, he did ask whether I was all right, but I avoided responding to him directly. I told him that I was confused and my thoughts were elsewhere, thinking about how much I missed his dad. Of course, he did not pry any further, being an obedient kid. I was, however, a bit unsure as to whether he would share the information with his dad. Budd usually telephoned about three times each day.

This incident had occurred just four days before I was to return to work after being on convalescent leave for about eight months. I pondered over how things would go once I returned to work. I wondered the most if I would be able to function as I did before, especially since my recent episodes of emotional desolation were beginning to occur more frequently. I was considered the go-to guru at work and was relied upon to do most any and everything while others always took credit for my work. Most of them took interest in knowing I was on their working teams. It never really bothered me, because I enjoyed being beyond dependable and revered as the cream of the crop.

I do not believe there is a previous boss of mine who would say that I did not perform exceedingly well, achieving high standards, regardless of any constraints. However, they might well add other perspectives, such as too straightforward and blunt. My prior performance competency was never an issue, but we all shared similar if not the same concerns surrounding my capability to perform at the same level as before. I had no doubt that my volatilities would become known soon, but presently only I knew of my current ineptness.

I returned to work and felt so out of place. The people I had previously interacted with appeared strange, and my new coworkers who acted cordial were less strange than most strangers. Weirdly, the people I should have felt comfortable being reintegrated with showed abnormal emotions, while those I had never met displayed hospitable normalcy. Perhaps this was based upon my own disconnection. Superficially, I preferred the company of strangers versus acquaintances, which made me feel even more unsettled. My anxieties grew more intensely, causing me to act fidgety, with negligent aspiration to integrate with an experienced or inexperienced team even though there were upcoming missions.

I appeared on edge because, as a leader, it is critical to trust your team as well as build trust among the team. My emotional behavior was unstable and alarming, raising concern that pressurized my uneasiness over whether a stranger would become acquainted with deficits and emotions that were unknown even to me.

The most pertinent upcoming mission involved major preparations for a dangerous combat missions deploying to Afghanistan. I became overwhelmed, allowing event preparation to bully my mind, oppressing my desire or duty to compose operational orders for soldiers to execute. Historically, executing a mission was never an issue for me as a competent professional; however, my competence was rapidly deflating like a bursting balloon. The room filled with strangers began to depress my mental confidence, enclosing me in a bubble that could pop at any minute. This process went on for about two days, and then an administrative clerk walked toward me to deliver the most startling news.

I was informed that I had been selected to work at another organization for a general, which was a promotion in a sense. I guess my excellent work record had earned me an opportunity that most people would have been excited about. Not me. I already knew there were too many unknowns to consider regarding the extent of my instability. I was really in disbelief, but of course the order to relocate was a formal written order, so there was little or nothing that I could do but comply. Frankly, since I was highly regarded as a stellar performer, I did not want to disappoint anyone, especially a high-ranking official. I proofread the orders and left work for the day to prepare so that I could report to my new job the next morning.

It was a job that would require extensive work hours, an unyielding commitment, and more sacrifice for my children. This was in no way possible. I now had an infant and was child-rearing as the sole parent of three. My husband was yet away, and I had absolutely no support system. I arrived home and talked with my two sons that evening, informing them that I had been directed to serve in a new position at a nearby location. Neither of them felt impacted; however, they understood that once again, hours upon hours would be spent away from them.

I tried my best to stomach this sudden change, even though I felt anxious and nervous. I went to bed early, because now my sunset would encounter my sunrise much sooner than before. I anticipated that my new schedule involved a ruthless schedule no matter the reason or the season. The expectation was to never be on time but to be early.

I tossed and turned most of the night, trying to digest the unspecified duties and the new and unfamiliar team. I was already fighting a battle to remain mentally fastened, because opening up and trusting others mattered more than one can imagine. I found it difficult to trust my peers, coworkers, and even leaders, Jobs with high visibility and prestige can make or break an officer's career, especially at my mid-grade level. At this point in my career, I had been a captain for about two years.

My previous two assignments involved working with all men, and that can be challenging. It was not because I felt less capable; oddly, some of the men I have worked alongside often were inept when it came to working with women who were more proficient than they. In my opinion, this was nothing new. Men practiced ego superiority to evade being professionally accountable, unlike women, who must produce quality work and perform at unparalleled levels to gain credibility.

The only difference with the military versus the civilian sector was that equal pay was cross-lateral, contingent to rank and time in service. However, this does not mean promotions toward earning that pay were offered with equal opportunity. Opposition lurked in the darkened corners. It was rare that men were challenged for this effort to camouflage workplace entitlement. I know firsthand, however, that it is no illusion. I outperformed my counterparts on many occasions and they never saw me sweat, but I did perhaps have to scream a time or two. At this precarious time, I did not care where or with whom I worked; I just wanted to be seen as competent, not crazy. My goal was to concentrate on my duties, since the immaterial matters would only further clog my congested life, swelling my anxieties. That is something I could not afford.

Chapter 8

Camaraderie Strangers

The next day, I arrived at my new job at a newly established organization located on a military installation. This new company was in a desert environment surrounded by multiple new buildings and shopping areas with beautiful military scenery. The building was a pleasant upgrade from my previous location, which was comprised of adjoining tan-colored trailers. This building had shiny waxed floors, artful hanging pictures, and a desk-seated soldier who greeted me with a, "Good morning, ma'am."

The building was about five stories high, with different sections handling various jobs in support of complex military missions. The soldier asked me for identification and proceeded to enlighten me as to the building's security measures. I had to be issued a coded identification badge authorizing access throughout the building.

I was excited but also nervous to travel throughout the facility after receiving my security badge. I was informed by the soldier that the office I needed to report to was on an upper level. I suffered from severe claustrophobia, and being in tight, enclosed places like elevators only heightened my isolation anxiety. However, as a warrior, there were expectations, and I knew them well. At this point, I had served over twenty years with a successful career.

Nervously, I proceeded toward the elevator and stepped inside, recognizing that I was all alone. I began to pray and ask

God to strengthen me during this ride and to prepare me for this opportunity to work with such highly regarded military leaders. Once I stepped off the elevator, I entered my new work area to discover that most of the desks were empty, with minimal busy-bee employees occupying the seats, which was slightly alarming. It was a red flag signaling that this job was being established ground up, and the undertaking to succeed was going to be extremely demanding. I paused, because I did not want to get ahead of myself and assume anything. I just wanted to be patient with the process of integration.

I sat at one of the desks awaiting verbal directives as to where to go, what to do, and who to speak with. Suddenly, I heard a familiar voice and saw a familiar face walk toward me. It was a dark-toned gentleman whom I had become acquainted with through my husband. He seemed as shocked as I was that I had been selected to work at this level.

No, I am not suggesting that he felt I was not experienced or deserving of the position. He was just surprised to see me. He was aware of my work record and achievements, since he had attended a job promotion for me several months earlier. We chatted briefly about our families; he asked about my husband and so forth. He did share that this job had many strains and a demanding schedule. This of course was one of my biggest concerns, and exactly what I not only anticipated but was also afraid of. I was beginning to become more perceptive regarding my emotional health, and I knew this transition would cause some level of eruption. I did not know when or where, but the brew was within me.

The dark-toned gentlemen asked me to walk around the office so that he could introduce me to my future team of coworkers. I obliged and began to explore the testosterone-filled atmosphere. At some point I realized that I had not been introduced to a single female employee or soldiers. I thought to myself, *This is odd!* However, I also thought that it could be misleading. *Perhaps they are out today or on a mission. Just be patient and wait to see.* I had lots of previous work experiences with all-male teams, and to be frank, it was getting old and too vexing.

After we were done touring the work section, a thunderous voice sounded: "Meeting in the conference room in fifteen minutes." This must be the head honcho, the commander. I assumed that someone would assure me it was, but there was no one present in my panoramic view, so I waited for the fifteen minutes to tick away. *Tick, tock.* The time seemed to creep by, and then people started down the aisle toward a huge room. This room was filled with about twenty large comfortable chairs, a massive projection screen, and two podiums. It was pleasantly well-organized room.

The big surprise was that there were nineteen men sitting at the table and the one me. At that point, what exactly do you say or think? I was not sure, so I sat silently baffled. Why was I always selected to work with an all-male team? I lived with all males prior to the birth of my daughter, and most my jobs consisted of all males. Was this coincidental, or was this purposely calculated?

Earlier, I mentioned that my pregnancy possibly created doubt of my competence as an expectant soldier for some, and now I imagined that this could be a way to ensure that they squeeze every drop from this mentally worn turnip, as my grandma often said. Perhaps not known to them yet was the uncertainty surrounding my health. The turnip had already withered, and drought prevailed.

Suddenly, the man in charge greeted me and asked me to introduce myself while sharing a piercing description of my duties and expectations as his assistant. The room was spinning like I had entered a merry-go-round, with my mind vacating my headless crown into a remote world. The only thing I heard was the chattering lips of flamboyant male voices going back and forth with silent expressions of agreement. I do not believe anyone even noticed me or that I had mentally separated from the room, being extant only in physical stature.

I snapped back once everyone stood up and rendered a salute, prepping me to return from my desolate whereabouts and likewise render a salute. The boss turned to me with a sturdy in-charge tone and said, "There's nothing on the schedule for today, so be prepared to get to work in the morning."

"Yes sir!" I replied. I gathered my things and swiftly walked out of the office to return to that frightful elevator. I trusted that no electrical outages or mishaps would occur to prevent my exit from this dreadful meeting, where I ear-throbbed my new work expectations.

I exited the building and rushed to my car. I sat there for a moment to gather my thoughts, wondering whether what had just occurred involved flashbacks of mental strain and suffocation. I was at a loss for words. I did not know how to connect my thoughts in-synch with my unresponsive actions. I did respond in absence of my reactions, but the expressions were not of my choosing or preference.

On my way home, I got a call from my husband, Budd. He was concerned about me returning to work, especially in light of the unexpected job transfer. Budd understood that, with him being away, I would inherit all the responsibilities at home and now at work, which was a major overload. Budd empathized with my position as my spouse and our children's father, but not always as a female supervisor. It wasn't until we married that he got to witness the maternal triumphs up closely.

My plate was now overwhelmingly filled with tasks and expectations which I had been annulled from for a long period— eight months, to be exact. Nevertheless, both Budd and I knew that with his absence, there was no one available to help lighten my load of responsibilities at either place, home or work. I did not share the episode of blankness while in the meeting with Budd. I did not want to disappoint him or add another side dish of worry to his plate, since he was already working as a contractor in a combat zone.

I pretended everything was fine and that I was looking forward to getting settled at my new place of work. I told him that I was released for the day, and I had to return to work tomorrow. My plan was to go home and get prepared prior to school dismissal for the boys. In addition to the boys, my parental duty had expanded, since I now had to pick my daughter up from daycare. I was exhausted just thinking of what was to come.

I needed to rest and recover before picking all the kids up from school. The goal was to regroup and analyze my approach, hoping to unveil to someone, even a stranger, what I was feeling. But who? After all, I was in a new setting, and I did not know anyone I believed I could trust with such sensitive information regarding my emotional state.

My mind was in a state of delusion, and I was trying to determine what to do. This situation made me feel abandoned by my old job, even though I had received a promotion. If and only if I had been given time to reintegrate before moving, perhaps I would have been able to express what I was struggling with. I would have felt more comfortable with someone more familiar to me as a person and a worker than complete strangers. So many people in my surroundings had changed jobs, positions, and locations, causing me to comprehend the gravity that life stands still for no one, whether you are here or there or up or down.

I awakened the following morning to prepare for work, hoping to become more engaged regarding my work duties. I dropped the boys off at each of their schools and my daughter to the daycare, and then I drove to work. It was awkward to be up and out of the house so early before dawn. Heck, even the sunrise seemed to awkwardly awaken me as it glistened through the window into my eyes. It felt great for me to be going back to work, and it made me feel revived. A job with a purpose not related to caring for children, chores, or paying bills, at last!

I drove steadily, not rushing but enjoying the transport as I glided down the busy lanes toward the entry to one of the military's largest installations. This was a tiring and tedious process, especially for the inspectors, who must deal with long lines waiting to enter. The identification check went more quickly than I expected, permitting me to gain access within seconds after my approach. I admired all the cars and people rushing to get to their units to ensure that they were accounted for by their leaders. I no longer had to do that; in fact, I had not reported to anyone for the past five years because of duties and being a military officer.

After driving about fifteen miles, I had arrived to my new

workplace. I retrieved my lunch and belongings, and I walked from the nearby parking lot. I had received my security badge the day prior, so I could proceed without strings toward the dreaded elevator once again. I was not feeling comfortable, so I asked someone nearby for directions to the staircase. A sharply dressed soldier in uniform pointed me in the right direction.

I quickly trotted off to the stairwell to hurry to the office. When I arrived, the room was half empty, but staff members were beginning to pour into the huge work area. It was filled with desk cubicles that were hidden by high walls, which made it difficult to visualize what lay behind the seated areas. This workspace provided much privacy, something my last office job did not offer.

The work call day was scheduled to begin at nine o'clock, when all VIPs (very important people) would report to work. The meeting room had something of a boardroom atmosphere, headed by not a president but in this case a commander. It was already around eight forty-five, so I had a mere fifteen minutes or so to get prepared. I started to practice some breathing techniques, breathing in and out to gain control of my heart pounding, which I assumed was due to workplace unfamiliarity.

The same loud thunderous voice from the day before echoed once again to call us to the meeting room. We all jumped up from our seats and headed in that direction, chatting quietly amongst each other until we were seated. The boss looked at me and proceeded to convey today's mission. I abruptly disappeared into darkness, even as I sat amongst a roomful strangers. There was no observable darkened closet, but instead, an obscure eclipsing cubicle with echoes of chaos. I do not believe that I vacated unconsciously but rather subconsciously to escape the subjection of ridicule. If anyone was to ask for my professional perspective and I stumbled, the backlash of ineptness may have indicated discontent with my capabilities by this environment overflowing with competency.

This very moment presented nothing but a hollow dark room where the muttering sounded like only a ricochet from a mountaintop rather than a voice giving orders nearby. GEMS was summoning me to a faraway place without any mission or expectation. It was figuratively rescuing me to report in an ambiguous spirit, which was something I had become physically and emotionally acquainted with.

The meeting proceeded without my participation; however, based upon the boss's request to see me after the meeting, he assessed that not all was good. He beckoned me to his office and closed the door after I sat in a brown leather chair. The chair suffocated my body with a hug of comfort that I so desperately needed at this very moment.

He looked at me and asked if anything was wrong. This was weird; it was the very first time I had been alone with this stranger who was my new boss. He told me that he asked me several questions during the meeting, and it appeared that I was not in tune with what was being directed to me. His soothing manner enabled me to openly say, for the very first time, "I am not all right. I need help. I can't do this." I began to share how my emotions and moods were like a roller coaster. Previously it had felt illegal to share my closet illness for fear of being shunned as if I had broken the law. I had broken an unspoken curse by giving a voice to this silent epidemic.

I also conveyed that my memory was unclear, and that I was restless, among other things. I was feeling depressed, with heightened anxiety about my surroundings. He realized that professional help was a command obligation and displayed a compassionate willingness to offer assistance. I sobbed with relief but also dreaded the reality that another stranger had been handed the key to my existence and control over my career fate. I was not sure whether he would handle it with care.

Two strangers—GEMS and a commander—now controlled my cerebral stability and the success of my career. I was clearly a fragile piece of bruised flesh, inside and out. The commander directed me to immediately report to the local military hospital so that a professional assessment could be conducted, hoping to determine what if anything was going on.

I arrived at the hospital alone, since I had driven myself without any assistance. However, I was given direct orders to report and provide a return call once I arrived. I was also told to provide a back brief as to the examining physician's assessments.

I waited for about ninety minutes in the emergency room prior to being screened. I hate hospitals; the smell, the appearance, and the feeling of aloofness inspire annoyance. Hospital staff in my experience often see patients as convicts of ill-health versus customers suffering from ailments. I rarely saw a provider who displayed empathetic bedside manners. Nonetheless, I waited to be seen and examined.

The doctor's assessment was not good, but indeed, that was not surprising. I was suffering from mental illness, and further examinations would be critical. The physician was suspicious of my sanity and feared that I was suicidal or even homicidal. Nonetheless, I convinced the hospital staff that I could not be placed immediately. My children had no caregiver, and my husband needed to be alerted so that he could return from Afghanistan.

I was immediately placed on restricted duty. As a parallel to this immediate measure, I was reassigned to a medical unit and given a profile for seventy-two hour that highlighted the urgency regarding my mental health. The physician's objective was to ensure an immediate appointment with a psychiatrist for an assessment for treatment, as well to keep me from returning to work.

The new command drafted a letter to forward to RISCOR, the company that my husband was employed by in Afghanistan, so that he could be on the next flight out. The doctor asked several times if I was a threat to myself or others: basically, if I was suicidal or homicidal. I dared not nor was I ready to divulge the bathtub episode. I was very hesitant but also afraid as to what would happen to me if I shared the incident—not to mention the risk to my three underage children.

I asked the medical liaison if I could return home, even though their desire was to admit me into a psychiatric facility. I strongly resisted based upon other anxieties like claustrophobia, memory loss, and fear of being overly medicated. I had heard some gut-wrenching horror stories in the past, and I was afraid. My understanding of the treatment of inpatient mental illness sufferers was unclear. I did not know whether psychiatric treatment was of mythical fiction or mystical fact.

I had visited a couple of mental health institutions in Kansas and Missouri about five years prior to my diagnosis, where both civilian and military patients were admitted. I did not witness compassionate care, nor did the patients display hope regarding their illnesses. Having witnessed this type of environment, I was concerned that I could be treated or feel the same.

The doctors agreed to my request to be released after I shared my verbal and emotional concerns about being sequestered against my will, even if it were for my mental benefit. I believe they wanted to prevent further anxiety, so they made an axis choice. Each had pros and cons. Though they were hesitant, the medical team was comforted by the knowledge that my husband, Budd, had received an emergency notification to return home from Afghanistan.

Budd was on the next flight and was expected to arrive back in Texas within twenty-four hours. I imagined that he was in a panic thinking about my psychological state as well as our children. My immediate response to the news that he was en route to the Kabul airport was a relief. Budd truly loved me!

I was emotionally defeated by all this medical news. However, I was even more concerned as to my captivity in a box, confining me in a place that made me feel silent but also shunned. I did not want to be a statistic, helping to reinforce societal perceptions and stigmas. The thought of being isolated from the norms of society was too sensitive to concur. However, by now it was clear that my psychological health was no longer an indeterminate diagnosis that I, the provider, or Budd could deflect. The best medicine moving forward was to recognize the existence of mental illness. But could I?

Chapter 9

Confirmation, My Strangest Diagnosis

T he medical examining physician—a high-ranking commander—
and I chatted for about thirty minutes to discuss my current
medical diagnosis. There was unspoken speculation about the state
of my health and career. I was not at all certain as to the next move
by me or them, so it was paramount to demonstrate professional
restraint regarding further inquiries, even though I was upset.
My focus was not to ask a boatload of questions, to avoid being
imperiled by something I could not cope with. I just wanted to
be cuddled away into someone's arms of shelter, secured in body-
armored protection.

The abruptness of too many details surrounding this alien
diagnosis literally frightened me to death. I felt alone and
deserted by an organization that I had given everything to,
while it reciprocated little to nothing in return. Previously, I
imagined that the military was the most cohesive organization
imaginable to protect me from any intrusive enemy, but I was so
misled. I do not believe that the military is at fault. Wars induce
many unimaginable afflictions, but the military is liable for the
inflictions of mediocre policy and protocols that inflicted life-
threatening detriments on me after the war. This may be an
opposing viewpoint regarding the protective safeguarding of

soldiers, but after two decades of service to country, who exactly is the contributing culprit?

Certainly, I am apprehensive about disclosing mixed feelings regarding who was the culprit or the enemy. It surely seems ungrateful to bite the hands about to feed me my most desperate meal for survival. I feared admitting that I was vulnerable, but even more so that I was a casualty, all because of my oath to serve. My plate was filled with an appetizer, main course, and dessert; however, the most desired part of the meal was my thirst for answers to quench a deeply dehydrated body. The nutrition that my body needed was too much for my stomach; its texture was too chewy and raw for my mind or body to absorb.

The physicians and the commander released me for the evening so that I could return to my home. I had to prepare for the medical journey that I would soon embark upon. I was provided with phone numbers to contact professional providers if my anxieties became urgent, necessitating emergency care. Certainly, I wanted to avoid any crisis with any unexpected provision of instantaneous therapy.

After being released, I returned home and received a phone call from my husband, Budd. He informed me that he would be arriving in about fifteen hours, since connecting flights had changed. Budd was so kindhearted and soothing during our phone conversation. He convinced me that everything would be fine and that I should remain calm. We chatted briefly about the doctor's diagnosis to avoid the forthcoming seriousness. However, I recall Budd expressing passion that reached from the blues above to the browns beneath. Budd said one thing and only one thing: "Susie, you are my everything, and everything you are to me!" It was uplifting to know that my partner would be at my side throughout this ordeal.

I hated that Budd had to leave his job, but I knew deep down that I needed him to be there to hold my hand. I needed physical cradling and shielding of my emotions from the pitfalls of devastation. Even though this was only a pre-diagnosis, I knew there was more news pending about this illness. Budd had been my in-sickness-and-in-health rock for almost two decades, and regardless of long odds from time to time, he never neglected to put my health as a top priority.

I was on edge the entire night awaiting Budd's return from overseas, tingling inside and out. I wondered while wandering room to room with anticipation whether he would have answers that no one else could possibly conceive of about my health. Budd knew me on a more personal level regarding my norms of expression, display of behavioral changes, and response to reactive incidents of rage than anyone else. A stranger assessing me might assume it was the norm, but in fact, it was abnormal. Budd could pick up on details that I might not have noticed but could also provide analytical depth.

I was hoping Budd's objectivity about my psychological state would offer more insightfulness. Budd was very perceptive when it came to my health, mood swings, and even ovulation. Oddly, he could predict my menstrual period better than me. His coupling connection oftentimes blew my mind as to how spot-on he was.

This tireless illness was beginning to impact my roots, my veins, and even my blood flow. It caressingly seeped into my brain stem, flooding me with interminable memories of darkness even during times of light. I could not remember things that were typical, things that did not require any thought—like, for instance, the company I worked for. I had forgotten or could not come up with the name for at least a minute or two. It was mind-boggling!

It was uncertain whether this was due to stress, depression, or the prior strokes impacting my brain's conception. Whatever it was or was not, it was affecting my mood, my thinking, and my behavior. I had vanished from a mental standpoint; only my physical being was in manifestation. The reality was that I had vacated in spirit, with only a visible shell that others were in acquaintance with from time to time.

My ability to process daily conversations and actions, or to be responsive without pause, was becoming extremely impaired. The stares that gazed at my window of sight showed tears that oozed anguish, all because of my numbness to react as society expected me to. This surreal expression of sadness captioned my fear and terror, causing me not to retort or respond. I did not want to grant unwanted perceptions to wreck my emotions any further in public; private scrutiny of self-interrogation was already a wreck inflicting mobile destruction.

I was now in a segregated box of solitude, which had me bumping into wall after wall, further imprisoning my mind. I felt as though my mind was surrounded, vanishing through egresses that slowly kept me chained no matter my struggles to escape. I was locked away, and I was hoping that Budd's key of love would release me from captivity, unlocking my emotional isolation sooner rather than later—perhaps tomorrow!

The morning was finally here. Today, my Budd would return. The doctor scheduled two appointments for me the day Budd returned from Afghanistan. There were vital yet additional evaluations that needed to be done. It was clear that a specific course of action was necessary to devise a therapeutic treatment plan to address a conceivable pre-diagnosis surrounding my mental illness instabilities. I expected something major to occur, but I had no expectations as to the nuts and bolts of the process. I asked minimal questions, if any at all, because I did not want to further baffle myself. For the past twenty years, my husband had attended all my doctor appointments, with the exception of my well-woman appointments, so his opinion was infinite.

Budd always inquired with spousal concern, asking for in-depth information more so than I. Budd had a medical background, so it was not at all an invasion of spousal-health privacy. He also took the kids to most of their doctor appointments, and cared for them whenever they were sick. I love my children dearly, but if they become sick, it is not me they seek, it is their dad.

My husband has always had such gentle, caring hands. Budd is a strong man who is never afraid to soften his touch when catering to the needs of his family, especially during sickness. My upcoming appointments revealed his extensive ability to caress fears surrounding my health.

When Budd arrived at the airport, he took a taxi home to mitigate stress for me prepping with the baby to retrieve him. I certainly appreciated this consideration. I wanted us to have time alone before the appointment, so I took the baby to the daycare, which was only about three minutes from where we lived. Once I returned from the daycare, the doorbell rang, and it was my beloved Budd. He grabbed me in his muscular arms so tightly that I felt like a smooshed pillow. His touch was so soft yet so full of comfort, compelling us both to be silent as our hugs expressed our solemn feelings.

It was about two hours before my appointment—enough time for Budd to shower, change, and grab a bite to eat. We spent a few moments of intimacy, and then we left for the appointment at the medical facility. It was time for me to be assessed and receive some medical advice.

Budd and I did not talk too intensely regarding my health. He did not want to get me aroused with any avoidable fears. His touch was comforting and his voice soothing. Budd turned, looked at me, and whispered with an air-kiss, "I am here, and things are going to be fine. Just trust God and then me." I felt like a watered flower that had been in a season of drought, with withering roots that suddenly felt rejuvenated.

Budd grabbed my hand as he parked the car. He pulled me in close and kissed my forehead. His soft kiss was deeply mesmerizing. It had been a few months since I had felt his intimate touch. Budd was a very composed, laid-back guy who rarely got upset about anything. His mission now was to protect me from my irrationality, calming upsetting waves no matter the situation. Although we did not know what to expect from the appointment, we did expect that we would be able to withstand this storm together, however precarious and unstable things got. My emotions were like the four seasons of the year: one day cold with no emotions like frosty winter; the next sunny like springtime, filled with darkness even though light; then hot as the summer sun with raging emotions, thirsting for hydration; and finally like falling leaves, silencing life while hoping for a resurgence.

We arrived at our appointment and approached the desk at the psychology department. We waited for our meeting so that we could see the assigned doctor who had my medical history in his notebook and my future in his hands. My hope was that my past marching would not impede my present strides in rebirthing a new walk toward a better future regarding mental soberness. It was like a drunkenness, but presumably only relatable because I felt unable to process any information.

Although I was not intoxicated with alcohol, I perhaps felt plastered because of some of the medications, which made me feel a bit off-pace. The intent was to stabilize my emotions and psychological imbalances with the ingestion of prescriptions like Maxalt-LT, Topermax, Lamictal, Effexor XR, Silenor, and Abilify, to name a few. Some of these can become addictive, with the likelihood of hallucinations.

Budd and I took a seat in the waiting area. Before long, I heard the physician call my name. My husband and I stood and walked toward the opened door, where we greeted a doctor with whom we were unacquainted. He was surprisingly compassionate and looked as if he already had a plan of action to begin my mental illness treatment. The three of us walked down a long hallway to get to his office and begin my psychoanalysis. The room was therapeutic, with a comfortable quietness that eased my nerves. My husband and I sat side by side on a couch while the doctor sat at his desk in a rolling chair, facing the two of us. I leaned into Budd's arm. I feared the complexity of imminent inquiries necessary to corroborate the doctor's evaluation.

We began to chat about my health, his assessment, and the recommended urgent medical management. Budd and I turned to each other with perplexed looks of uncertainty—for me, over the effects of my fading image, and for Budd, over the effects of my treatment with impending concerns to my health. Budd did not sense me to be a different person, but perhaps he understood that the personalities inside of me were diverse and impacting the health of the person he knew.

I was not ashamed of anything within these walls of solace—primarily because it was a private domain where I could be freed from perception without criticism. There were so many thoughts surfing through my mind, none of which I understood clearly or with the capacity to openly express, so I just blubbered. Budd grabbed me in preparation for the doctor's next sentence, supposing it was going to be difficult for me to ingest. Indeed, ingesting this medical language made me nauseous and prevented me from digesting the scope of the medical diagnosis.

The doctor shared his multilayered multiple diagnoses, which blew our minds even further. I felt bullied by all these medical terms and discoveries that the psychiatrist revealed. He informed us that I was suffering from severe depression, severe anxiety, memory loss, and PTSD. I did not know how or what to think at this point, so I just sat mutely watching the movement of his lips, which flapped without sound. My mindless ineptitude had begun to melt away my once-mindful subconscious.

The next thing I remember is that the doctor recommended that I be committed to an inpatient mental hospital facility to assess my mental state even more closely for some undisclosed amount of time. I suddenly rebelled with chatter, screaming, and weeping.

"No!" I cried. "No, I am not going to be admitted to any facility! I am not crazy, even though I do not know what is going on at this very moment in life."

We sat there for the next thirty minutes as the doctor tried to convince me to agree to hospitalization and I tried to convince him that I could not deal with another layered wall of isolation or seclusion. I sensed isolation from the outside world might led to sequestration of not only my mind and emotional state but now my enfeebled carcass. The room went mute as I wiped tears with a Kleenex that the doctor placed in my palm. He exited the room to confer with another medical professional as to what to do about my resistance to be in treatment isolation.

Budd tried hard to convince me that everything would be all right. However, he also knew that I had recently begun suffering from another anxiety, which was claustrophobia. If I was placed in a confined environment without freedom to roam, it might prove more harmful than helpful. Ultimately, movement without free will would not be good.

I had become frightened of elevators, windowless rooms, tight-fitting clothing, and plane travel. I would undergo extreme panic at the notion of being restrained physically, visually, and bodily. It was like being in bondage, and there was no way to escape. My fleshly existence was metaphorically out of touch. These emotional reactions arose out of thin air like an unexpected storm, with no advance forecast.

I recall purchasing an expensive dress from a very upscale boutique. The dress was gorgeous, and I could not wait to try it on. I had recently lost about fifteen pounds of ill-desired voluptuousness, and I was looking thin and attractive. The dress was a cream beige-like color and very stylish. When I tried the dress on, however, I began panting with panic, as if I felt suffocated by the dress surrounding my neck and arms. There was a zipper on the right waist of the dress, but it would not to bulge. I panicked and ran outside of my apartment, ripping the dress completely off my skin.

I looked around once I had shredded the dress into pieces to see if anyone witnessed this alarming incident. I felt like the clothing was attacking me and choking my airway, leaving me unable to breathe. I responded like I was an animal in a cage, battling to defend myself from this helpless fabric of a dress. This was just another assertion that something was wrong and not right with my mental state, causing disturbing reactions without sanity. This incident was not shared with the psychiatrist, for it was too embarrassing a sign of the spiraling of my emotions.

The doctor returned to the treatment room to deliver the team of evaluating psychologists' decision. It was clear that I had to abide by their ruling if I wanted to get better. The decision was to admit me for intensive outpatient treatment at a mental hospital for a six-month period. The doctor made it clear that intense therapy, medication, and counseling were vital for me to regain my self-identity as a functioning being.

The doctor shared that I had forty-eight hours to report to the facility and be processed into the outpatient treatment program. He suggested that we visit the facility immediately following my appointment, so that I could begin my transition. I was no longer afraid of the treatment but more afraid of being locked away if I arrived at a facility with uninformed professionals who did not grasp the gravity of my panic attacks. These alien psychiatrists and medical professionals had the authority to change my projected treatment plan with no input from me or even Budd.

Budd and I drove to the facility, which was in New Mexico. It was tucked away in a remote area but not too far away from civilization. We drove around the facility and then parked the car. I noticed soldiers walking around the compound with escorts and felt a bit unnerved, but at ease knowing that my comrades were at the facility as well.

Budd asked me to stay in the car as he went to get information from one of the escorts as to the in-processing location. Budd was pointed in the direction of a white medical office building that looked detached from the patient area. I was nervous but ready to discover more about the place that would become my mental refuge for the next six months. It was important that I be receptive rather than ejective, so that I could at last take the first step toward recovery.

Budd retrieved the paperwork but returned accompanied by a medical escort to rally me from the car. I was polite but apprehensive. Nevertheless, I complied and joined them as we walked to the building. I became acquainted with the facility surroundings and the staff, although I was not being formally in-processed for at least another forty-eight hours. I felt like I had committed a crime, and the crime was self-inflicted. The misconduct had caused me to lose control over my own life decisions because of the ravaging ill-will of my mental health.

My behaviors had undergone a transformation, which was evident by the professional assessments. I was not in agreement or disagreement with those results. My desire was to understand the conflicting emotional changes that I was aware of, but unaware of the root cause. The staff was cordial in providing explanations of different processes, procedure compliance, and daily treatment routines. The plan was that I would be assigned to this facility for six long months, eight to ten hours each day, five days a week. The alternative would have been admission as an impatient, twenty-four hours a day, seven days a week!

Budd and I completed the walk-through and returned to the car with various informational pamphlets. I looked at them briefly, but frankly, it was kind of depressing. We drove away from the facility, glimpsing a town kicking off grand openings for different stores. Budd pointed toward stores that I liked to shop as well new ones. He was hoping to alleviate my mental contravention, pausing the focus on my impending treatment with something more pleasing to a woman's brain: shopping!

We noticed an ice cream parlor and, since it was a warm sunny afternoon, stopped for some flavor-sampling. It was rare that I could enjoy something as simple as an outing for ice cream. I was mostly too frozen by society, believing annoying perceptions might melt my taste. It is not clear that I acted unusual, but presumably I portrayed societal detachment through gesturing, where oftentimes I failed to communicate through visual contact. At the ice cream parlor, I tastefully ogled all the different types and flavors. Finally, I decided to get yogurt with a waffle cone. Waffle cones were my favorite ice cream treat. The yogurt was delicious!

Budd does not eat ice cream or yogurt because of milk allergies, so he chose a flavored drink. We sat for about twenty minutes and enjoyed our servings, relishing the moments of intimate conversation and privacy. We connected like two peas in a pod, appreciating the comfort of being close once again. Our union of love was real, and neither of us had to say a word. Our eyes transferred our feelings and the purity of our emotions. When couples have been together long as we have, their thoughts seamlessly merged as spouses, friends, and advocates for my well-being.

The forty-eight hours was quickly approaching for my outpatient treatment to begin at my new home away from home. I was less apprehensive with fear and anxiety but still curious about these uncharted waters now flooding my reluctance. Nevertheless, I was becoming more optimistic and focused on health so that I could become mindfully present for my family. The good thing was that I had Budd with me for the first five days of treatment, which made it bearable. He catered to me with compassion and support.

When I arrived to the facility on my first morning, an unexpected wave of nervousness surfaced; however, I was committed and ready to begin this journey toward recovery. I entered the building where I would spend long days and many hours. The area felt drab and cold, with a sense of stillness wandering from face to face as I stared into a room filled with bleakness. There were about fifteen people standing, sitting, and kneeling in a squared space with limited mobility. The noise was light, with muffled chatting about nothing much, where the ill were trying to project a sense of relevance with dialogue.

I was flabbergasted by the number of people in the room, but also the display of visible mental illness injuries to my fellow comrades. We all shared the commonality of mental wounds, seeking recovery from an injury that was killing us insidiously. Perhaps many of us were wounded by a nonpiercing bullet that ricocheted after inflicting post-traumatic fears and stressors. There were no traces of skin permeation, but somehow these combat wounds seemed incurable, stifling the livelihood of many veterans.

It seemed we were all dying emotionally, struggling to clot

internal wounds from grave bleeding deep within. The wounds I observed with my own eyes were like being on a battlefield of fleeing allies trying to escape torturous enemy fire. I thought, *Oh my God, the war is yet ongoing, but on a different battlefield.* I saw frightened, injured warriors who were emotionally destroyed by adversarial attacks. The suffering was riveting, because I now had an up-close and personal perspective as to societal stigmas concerning mental illness and disorders.

I witnessed my peers who were clearly medicated exhibiting slurred tonguing and rocking back and forth in feeble positions as some paced the room with visible fidgeting. I also noticed a staff member in the vicinity, which I later learned was a security measure. Certainly, the staff and other patients were fearful as well as attentive to protect themselves from the fray of violently ill patients. This sight of illness was initially blinding, but it was also confirmation that I too had a fluctuating degree of illness.

I do not know what any of their mental illness diagnoses were, although I speculated about some of them. My reality was becoming clear as to the gravity of mental illness and its impact to my recovery. I hoped that whatever was causing memory lapses and emotional discord, treatment would provide therapies to cure me. I did not want to stare at my comrades, but the sight of psychological hollowness was devastating to witness.

I was in an unpredictable environment filled with fears, behavioral divergence, and unchosen isolation, which was initially surreal to comprehend. I had been caged in a room with people suffering like me but very much unlike me in many ways. We were mirrored in the essence that all of us were suffering from mental illness. Nevertheless, we were matchless in the fact that our illnesses were dissimilar, the severity was diverse, and prescribed treatment was individually distinct. I suppose the complexity of mental illness made us believe we were different, but it was clear that we were much the same. I sat there perplexed, ingesting all this improbability, when suddenly a comrade approached me. He introduced himself, and we began chatting about little to nothing.

After being evaluated for three days, I began to inhabit my setting with receptiveness and greeted my treatment with a welcome. This treatment was like an emotional roller coaster of multidimensional assessments jumping from one ride to the next. Initially, I was provided with an increased dosage of medication, one-on-one counseling with a therapist, group counseling with my veteran peers, and cognitive therapy. I also had to partake in physical fitness activities each day to relax and sustain a level of fitness that was a military requirement. This schedule of intense therapy lasted for about nine hours daily as an outpatient participant.

On the fourth day, I was met with cheerful optimism by a young Hispanic nurse. She told me that the doctor was scheduled to meet with me so that a more aggressive treatment plan could be implemented. Up to this point, my mental health status had only been a matter of speculation. Now, after days of medical evaluation by a team of psychiatric professionals, my truth was emerging into the dismal air. I did not know what to expect, nor did I believe it would be what previous doctors hypothetically diagnosed. Regardless of what my mental intuitions materialized in theory, my lack of emotional gravity was symptomatically opposite, exposing the realization that my bodily synchronization had suffered some vulnerable breakages.

The nurse exited from a back-office room where patients would meet the doctor for individual counseling and therapeutic treatment on a biweekly basis. This would be my initial meeting with an all-inclusive behavioral evaluation merged from the previous hospital and the current mental-health treatment facility. My name was called, so I stood up and followed my escort to the area in which the session would take place.

There were three medical professionals in the room, including a doctor who had more credentials than I cared to pronounce. Clearly, he was qualified to delivery whatever diagnosis he was primed for. A second opinion is always recommended; this would be perhaps the fourth medical opinion, but a more comprehensive one.

The doctor greeted me and introduced himself with a smile. He had several pages of paperwork, and he proceeded to release the most heartbreaking news imaginable for someone like me who was in denial of my mental state of mind. The doctor looked me straight in the eye and delivered the blow like so:

"You have undergone massive mental traumas, emotional disconnects, behavioral changes, and a combat-induced distress that has produced psychological overload with the inability to functionally cope."

I had clearly been blinded by denial, but after stepping out of darkness, my eyes began to see more clearly in the light. I was in shock, but not total shock, since I had prepared myself for what seemingly was the worst. Although it wasn't the worst news, neither was it the best news. I was diagnosed with memory loss, severe anxiety, severe depression, PTSD, as well as two other illnesses— bipolar disorder and panic disorder—that were later unveiled.

I have been taught to not allow anyone full disclosure of my internal being. It was no different now, even in illness. It was critical to deter further effects of the illness, so full disclosure was paramount to achieving my recovery. I sat numb for only a moment. Even though I was ill, I did not want to return to my health treatment group weakened by the news, especially since I was the second-highest-ranking individual in the room. I had to consider what junior subordinates would think of me as a leader, even though I was not currently in a leadership role but in a position of vulnerability.

The military had been my lifeline for over two decades, and I was not ready to sever the lines. However, I was ready and determined to evaluate these physical traumas—mental demands that I believed were induced by a military career and possibly my genetically branched tree. However, my hope now was to discover what contributed to my mental health decline. Was it sudden or a lengthy deterioration? Either way, I now had a diagnosis, a therapeutic management team, and a handful of bottled prescriptions to accompany me on my travels.

The only issue was, what direction would I travel first? Would I own this diagnosis? Would I commit to treatment for progressive recovery, or would I suffocate my livelihood by self-medicating my illnesses and disorders? Trust me when I say this was no easy task nor stress-free choice, but at least I had options.

Each of us is birthed into the world before we come into our existence of being relevant, not knowing what will occur before or after birth. My journey to discover what sidetracked my health led me to examine the tree from which my fruit had fallen. Was it my mother, my father, or just perhaps life that had led to unexpected congestions that necessitated removal to proceed?

Chapter 10

Strangely Rooted by Uncultivated Fruit

I am the third child, middle child, third daughter, but only sibling who honored the request of my veteran father, who died only months after returning from the Vietnam War. He was cheated out of life but also cheated out of fatherhood of four young children— three daughters and one son. My last two siblings were born after his death.

There is a total of six of us siblings, but one of my beloved siblings had struggled in vain for weeks to defeat death, battling a demonic illness: a rare brain cancer. The brain is unbelievably resilient yet so fragile; I know firsthand how vulnerable it is. This part of backpedaling my birth and past is painful. I am on a exploratory voyage, traveling paper-trail roads from one country to another to ponder why some branches rooted survive and others wither.

How is it that storms of rain, snow, hail, and extreme heat can damage the livelihood of some while others thrive to produce more fruit? It's amazing to ponder but more amazing to comprehend that no two branches are the same. Yet they are similar, with their own identity of physicality and strength.

I am one of five known branches rooted by my father and one of six rooted by my mother. These two rooted me, but one is an anonymous seed who did not get the full reaping of his seeds. However, they would grow without that stranger's nurturing. I too am a stranger, but not as strange to life as my father. My self-imagery is a painful reminder of my father because of our physical resemblance. I was blessed with my father's hazel-brown eyes, his skin tone, his lips, and perhaps some of his unknown talents. What a mystery it is to wonder at one's genetic similarities to someone one can only speculate about, as if a spectator versus a paternal relative.

I knew very little about this strange man for forty-five years simply because I was barely two years old when he died in a car accident. My father was a teenager—only nineteen years old—when he was drafted to serve his country. He spent three tours in a combat zone. For years, my mother evaded discussions about my father's childhood and short-lived adulthood as well as his legacy as a combat veteran. It's hard to imagine, but my father's life was hardly ever discussed in any manner, even by his mother and siblings.

My father's family lived only about thirty miles away from us. I presumed that my mom was so distraught that she proceeded with her life as a single parent, rearing four of this mysterious man's children with little to no assistance from his family. My mother shared something special with me about my father that led to my career choice. It was over twenty-five years ago that my father's last wish was that one of his children pay him homage by joining the military to serve our country by choice rather than being drafted. My family assumed that it would be my brother, the only son birthed by my dad and mom. Unfortunately, my brother took a different path, and the road made a U-turn back to me, the youngest daughter.

My mom decided to honor my service in fulfillment of my father's request by giving me his military honors, including his burial flag. It was touching and surprising—a moment that I will forever cherish. My mom beckoned me to a room while she was visiting from out of town. Three of my siblings were also there when she pulled the flag from a white soft wrapping that looked like a pillowcase. The flag glistened with sentiments, even with the reflection of a small brown stain. None of us knew what was about to happen, and then suddenly, my mom placed the flag in my arms and said, "This is yours. Your father would have been so proud of you!"

I teared up and replied, "Thank you. This means so much!"

My siblings were speechless. Not a word was spoken, but their teary silence and smiles corroborated their feelings. This was shocking but so amazing—reaping a special endearment of such heroism regarding the end of my father's life and career. This was a symbol of patriotism miles apart from the injustices of America in the insidious jungles of Vietnam. Initially, I thought my other siblings would be upset, but they were very understanding and recognized that it was the appropriate recognition of my sacrifices to honor a stranger who was mostly a foreign father.

Although I refer to him as a stranger, I wanted to learn more about him, since our paths were interconnected, more so than any of my siblings. Family members would often say, "You look just like your father." I was named after his mother, which further corroborates that he too believed that I got most of my genetics from his side of the family tree. My discovery began when my mother came to visit me years ago and wanted to inquire about her military spousal benefits. I decided to research various requirements, discovering things that no one in our family ever knew about that stranger as my father, as a husband, and as a son.

I requested my father's military records, and after receiving document after document, I became enthralled and determined to learn even more. I was absorbed by my father's military records, which provided insight as to his service as well as his life prior to military service as a thriving citizen. My father graduated high school at the top of his class, which was a rarity for a black man in the South in the mid-1960s. I was proud of this accomplishment, and now I was determined to read every word on every page.

I routinely called my mom and shared interesting details with her. I was sure that not even she knew her husband as I had come to know him while serving his country. Per my mom, my father was a caring man who loved his children dearly, but he was also a man who liked to socialize and party. My father often indulged in the street life when away from home. This information did not change my perception of him; after all, he's my father but also deceased. I am an adult, so I understand fleshly imperfections, for neither am I perfect.

I was searching to enrich my understanding by tracing the root from whence I was seeded. I was a legacy branch of my father. Was the soil adulterated? We know that not all soil is healthy, although we do not realize it until the fruit appears putrid, causing degeneration. I had researched, read, examined, and processed so much information that I was becoming fatigued. Suddenly, my father's medical records with detailed information surfaced. I was in shock, and now I would perhaps find the answers to my questions involving the deterioration of my mental health.

My father served three Vietnam tours, buried in the jungles in some of the most dangerous areas because of his military occupation, expertly firing along with his units of assignment. He was overtly exposed to different chemicals, poisons, and other health hazards but had no way out. He had been drafted to serve our country. Most soldiers had to succumb to death of freedom because of the Vietnam War, whether by physical jailing if you refused to go to Vietnam or perhaps emotional jailing for life after returning from Vietnam. I believe my father received a double sentencing of jailing: physical and emotional. What a sacrifice for your country! So people, please believe when I say on behalf of my father, myself, and other veterans, that freedom is not free!

After serving three tours and constantly being away from his family, my father casually exited the military, but he had no idea— or did he?—what being in a war zone had done to him. I was the only child birthed by my dad and mom after his initial exposure to those highly toxicities while in Vietnam. The medical reports said my father suffered dramatically, with lesions on his stomach and back; his limbs ached with neurological debilitative demise. Stressing and struggling to cope, my father turned to alcohol and drugs. Presumably, this was the beginning of his breakdown and disconnect prior to returning home from the war. My father out-processed his duties in California as an active-duty soldier but joined a reserve unit in Louisiana.

My dad was never the same after Vietnam—mentally, emotionally, physically, or spiritually. I believe he had too many demonic strangers like GEMS disrupting his ability to reintegrate into a society where he struggled to cope. There were no offerings of therapy, treatment, reintegration to society or family, or employment opportunities. There was no one to understand the gravity of his struggles.

My father had become uprooted. He was dying and wilting at the hands of his own country's inadvertent antagonistic opposition to those who serve without consent. Every tree goes through its season, but it can only withstand the storm if cared for properly, with the reciprocation of refurbishments. My father saw no way out or in, so he began to isolate himself, much like soldiers had to do during the war to protect and secrete their emotions. It suggests that his courage was not strong enough to endure the psychological changes that he was experiencing.

After the discovery of this data, I decided to share the evidence with my mom to gauge her perspective. For the first time ever, my mom released her suppressed burdens to share the things she witnessed in my father's behavior after returning from Vietnam. He had become mentally and emotionally unhinged; he was wracked with fears, anxieties, war delusions, and memory loss, along with physical injuries all over his body. These rashes were also on his face; just imagine not only feeling like war ravaged your life but to also gaze at your face and see the distresses of war staring back at you daily.

My warrior-father started to drink heavily, smoke marijuana, abuse his family with rage, and vacate the home for days at a time, returning as if nothing had transpired. He also landed himself in jail on several occasions because of his spiraling behaviors. It was clear to even my mom that this rooted tree had gone through some storms, impeding his ability to replant himself in a soil of normalcy or liberate himself after direct warfare.

The pieces of the puzzle were beginning to not only fit but to also establish the possibility of genetic seeding from parent to child. I was on a predestined mission to record a step-by-step account of my father's demise. I backtracked to fast-track the discovery of my own health demise. I had honored this stranger's request, and now it was my turn to return to a war zone much like my father's, risking the stability of my own life. Was my destination preordained and commanded by my heavenly father, or was my destination routed to a path of destruction followed by my earthly father? I had abided by my father's service request, but now I was about to find myself fulfilling that request with a depth of consequence I had never anticipated.

I joined the military months after Desert Shield and Desert Storm in the early 1990s to begin my endeavor to honor the strangest but the most bonded man I know, my father. A mom and dad's most sacred bond is and will always be a child, even when they part ways by choice or by circumstance. I had a long, challenging, and rewarding career as a service member for over two decades. I won, lost, broke even, and sometimes even tired depending on the mission at hand. I have no regrets over serving my country, but I often regret some of my choices in building reciprocal relationships.

I served in a multitude of positions, performed an array of jobs, and cared for the welfare of multiple troops, but the most rewarding thing for me was the career advancement or achievements of someone I directly led. In my opinion, my individual achievements far exceeded what I ever expected, simply because my goal was to serve a term, not to entrench a career. However, after many years, numerous duty stations, multiple bosses, and inevitable standards, I finally completed that fatherly oath of service.

Service to my country and my father has led me to reevaluate my contributions of self-depreciation in a context that is vital to my mental health recovery. Genetics played a role in ways unknown, but there were many other factors, including physical traumas faced head on. In particular, there were three instances that come to mind of direct brain combat—three accidents involving collisions where the impact was directly cerebral. I was the driver each time.

The first incident was a head-on collision while driving at five in the morning to a military formation of physical activities referred to as PT. I was traveling to work, and a car was approaching with no lights on. The light was green for us both to travel in our north and south directions. I had to make a left turn onto the interstate but failed to yield for the oncoming vehicle because of its lack of lighting. This caused a head-on collision after which, for the first time in my life, I was silent. I lay on the ground unconscious; my six-year old son sat crying as I was pulled from the car bay a stranger.

My son was in the car with me so that I could take him to daycare on my way to formation. He was unharmed by the accident, while I was rushed to the hospital by ambulance. Budd and I were told that I possibly was paralyzed from the waist down and might not walk again. I had only been married about thirty days. Certainly, this was not what a newlywed husband wanted—a disabled wife from some freak accident. However, God did not see fit for this accident to disable my life. It was due to his mercy that I walked out of the hospital.

The second brain trauma occurred during my travels in a small town in Mississippi. I was preparing to deploy to Iraq and needed to take my children to my mom in Mississippi. I was traveling with my mom and sister on an interstate at a high rate of speed but within the speed limit of 75 miles per hour as posted along the interstate road. Suddenly, a jumping buck appeared in my peripheral vision, and before I knew it, his eyes met mine. I gazed directly into a wondrous land of lanes fearing the safety of my recently purchased car as well several bypassing cars inadvertently heading toward me but somehow avoiding me. The deer went sliding off the car; the only thing I could hear was screaming and panicking from my mom and sister.

There were other cars on the road, so I had to keep my composure in steering the car as straight forward as possible, with throbbing feet that cramped as I strained to control the car's braking motion. This accident was deathly fearful! Unequivocally, I believe it also perhaps created destabilization of my brain with the interconnecting speed and impact directly at my side window. I walked away intact physically, but I question perhaps whether a demise had begun mentally and emotionally because of undetected traumas of my mental capacity over the years, especially with the proximity of these possible brain injuries or concussions. Doctors provided numerous possibilities for the cause of my mental illness, but there was never denial of my suspicion. The concurring validation by each assessing professional health-care provider was that my brain had undergone physical trauma and distress.

The third head trauma occurred while in combat. I was a leader accompanying one of my subordinates during a life-threatening mission, convoying from one location to another. The soldier driving the vehicle panicked and could not get the vehicle to shift gears during a high threat of vulnerability. I jumped out of the vehicle to take over, because the halt of our vehicle not only placed us within enemy territory but risked the lives of over two hundred other personnel. I did not think twice; I suppose my adrenaline was going so fast that no thought of fear was contemplated.

As a leader, I had countless responsibilities prior to this convoy, resulting in working wee hours in the night after staging loads of vehicles. My responsibility was to ensure that all command directives were completed as well as make sure the soldiers I led were combat-ready. There were three individuals assigned to ride in my vehicle, which was called an LMTV. One of the soldiers was a newly assigned Asian troop member who had not earned his driver's license. This was not the norm; it was mandatory to be licensed, but because of time constraints and language barriers, the system faltered. This mishap put me in a predicament; I had to drive, command my platoon, and be ready to execute fire support if necessary during the convoy.

I was tired, overwhelmed, and heavily relied upon with task after task; nonetheless, I had to react regardless of the level of distress. This vehicle was of massive weight, and it was filled with priceless equipment that was essential in providing medical care during the deployment. Once I took the wheel, there was no time to stop or make any readjustment between me and the previous driver.

I was extremely exhausted. I continued to drive for two to three hours. At some point I must have dozed off, and I awakened to a fearsome catastrophe. I was not cognizant and perhaps even in a deep dream from which I was awakened by screams and people yelling. The vehicle was surrounded by a 360-degree perimeter of security. We were in combat, but more than that, we were in a territory with high enemy threats. I had rammed this massive truck into the rear of the vehicle in front of me, which was only a quarter of the LMTV's weight and size.

I heard people yelling "Stop, stop!" but I continued to ram the truck, which suggests that I was yet unaware as to the circumstances. Once I realized what was happening, it frightened me into anxiety, because what was next? It took about thirty minutes to remove the vehicle buried underneath my truck, employing the muscle of about twenty men. It was fear-provoking for those pulling security but also for those attempting to free the vehicle.

There was lots of damage to the vehicle that I rear-ended. Sadly, this vehicle was carrying the hospital surgery equipment to treat wounded casualties. My stress was trifold: incurred injuries, operable vehicle, and financial liability for cost of the vehicles.

I believe that the totality of these three accidents led to the inception of brain trauma and distress. It is certainly possible that cerebral destabilization occurred because of the incidental impacts of multiple speed, power, and weight. I never even considered these three incidents until years later, when I began to experience mental illness. These cerebral confrontations were clear contributors to my memory loss, even though that was not detected at the time. Obviously, a disease lies dormant without detection until the symptoms become too much for inward restraint and must be outwardly released.

Work demands are another factor contributing to my brain's capacity to become overstretched without the elasticity to bounce back. The demands of work and play often dictate mental responsiveness in a myriad of ways, determining whether the aftermath will have any lingering effects. For me, I have always been an achiever who strived for success by exceeding—not just meeting—a standard. I truly believe that my desire to be extremely proficient as a dedicated soldier caused undue stress in my life, as it certainly alleviated stress for others. I was eager to undertake my coworkers' tasks, my family's baggage, and my friends' issues, ignoring the impact it all had on me.

These thresholds of straining servitude were often without boundaries, proffering no antidote to cure the mind from overloading chaos. Ironically, there were choices in the matter involving certain family and friends' issues, but I wanted to be the savior of all. It was different for work, because for work, ignoring my sworn commitments was not only impossible but also not plausible. I worked tirelessly, sacrificing so copiously but reaping so modestly with measureless voids inside and out. That does not mean that I failed or was not successful in my career, but clearly, I was overtaxed mentally and emotionally.

I can now admit, years later, that the dictates of others depleted me. My glass always appeared either half full or half empty; nonetheless, it was always less than expected. The lesson that I learned throughout my mental illness was not to allow myself to be relied upon too often but instead to be depended upon; it freed me from being tied to the demands of others with the capacity to step up when necessary and step out when I needed to. When one totally relies upon someone else to do something, it implies an inability to do it oneself, but depending on someone suggests trusting that person to do something although you are capable.

Life became less arduous when I learned to be depended upon instead of relied upon. Teamwork is infectious and counteracts self-centering of individual superiority. Additionally, other risks are mitigated that lessen stress, failures, and exertion of preeminent power. The probability to overburden one person and not the team minimizes the opportunity to celebrate shared success. Learning to collectively share the spotlight is the best way to illuminate efforts of each contributor.

A good team embraces small and large contributions. The

essence of working together will interchange profoundly from one task to the next, revealing a conservative or reflective energy. Each of us must seek inspiration that fills our own darkened spaces. No matter the room's perceived luminosity, it can become blockaded by a dimness that is much darker than it appears. I needed my life to be lit with a spiritual phenomenon, renewing my darkened spirit.

I was starting to learn that life was about creating memories and moments, cementing life during life and life after death—one's legacy. It's unequivocally what you leave behind, not what you depart with, that counts. The enlightenment that I yearned for was not only to see my surroundings but also to relate to my environment. I was blinded by emotional darkness without the capacity to comprehend the touch of what I was feeling.

Mental illness has the propensity to erode many facets of one's mental capacity—a telltale sign that early detection is essential whether anyone believes it, fact or fallacy. However, no one who suffers can afford to ignore mental illness's inauguration into existence. On the contrary, even if it proves not to be related to mental illness, it could be the beginning of a journey one doesn't expect to travel, much like that of my sister, who was diagnosed with a rare brain cancer.

I discovered that my youngest sister suffered nearly three years from severe headaches, memory loss, and anxiety that contributed to a more life-threatening yet debilitating illness with untreatable odds to beat. I believe she feared not only seeking medical help but also what would be revealed. Painstakingly, after years of suffering, she discovered that a rare brain cancer had invaded her body, causing a multitude of ailments contributing to cerebral dysfunction.

I am in no way suggesting that the rare cancer, glioblastoma, had a substantial connection with mental illness or disorders. However, I am candidly suggesting that mental illness can erupt in complex facets because of brain activities that are incalculably complicated. These varying facets possibly led to my sister's and my unsuspected illnesses, which caused a lapsing of the brain's functionality. For one reason or another, an intervening disruption clearly impacted our mental responsiveness. Our family's sunshine recently lost the battle against brain cancer, but she won a victory by being freed—staring death in the face day in and day out.

My mental illness concerns began much like hers: with confusing headaches and memory loss. I am overwhelmingly humbled that I had access to resources that afforded early detection and treatment. Perhaps I am one of the lucky ones; my military service authorized medical resources to be within my reach. Not everyone has the benefit of accessible health care as an American. I believe my sister's suffering led to comprehension regarding my fading mental health. Something was not only un-centering balance but everything was either too far left or too far right, depending on the situation.

As for my sister, through whom I live vicariously, there was obviously cloudiness blocking rays of sunshine that signaled bleakness. When storms of life are raging and you are ill-prepared, without protection, exposure of the impact will eventually come full circle. It was unfortunate that my sister could not afford preventive or early-detection medical services, but that may have led to a more sinister fear: denial and rejection when a doctor gives a true diagnosis. I wonder if full discovery surrounding her illness impacted her mental capacity to process the devastation that cancer would wreak on her body.

I clearly remember the day that my family, with the exception of my ill sister's children, found out that she had been diagnosed with brain cancer. My sister informed the family that she would call us after the doctor's diagnosis and that everything would be fine. She was still in the hospital for about three days after discovery of a tumor. At this point, it was not diagnosed as brain cancer but only a small brain tumor.

We all gathered at one of my sister's homes in Kansas City. I was returning from a football camp that was in Ohio, but after hearing the emotional fears, I rerouted my trip to Kansas City. I wanted to be there as family to support my sister and those of us frightened about the forthcoming diagnosis. My sister Sandra called, and the phone was placed on speaker so we could hear the news simultaneously.

Sandra revealed her heartbreaking news: "I have a rare brain cancer, and the doctor has given me only six months to live!"

We were in shock. We all sobbed, and the tears and pain stunned our souls inside and out. It was devastating! My ill sister was so calm and optimistic, with a melodic voice as of an angel, delivering tunes to her song of life. I cannot even imagine the solemn demeanor and her mental and emotional poise to be so spiritually tranquil.

We all suspected that this would be an uphill battle. My sister wanted desperately to defeat this foe, opting to undergo brain surgery two or three times to remove the tumor, but its location was too awkward and its impact too powerful. Her detriment alerted me that I needed an immediate assessment to get a medical perspective as to my emerging medical condition. I am forever grateful yet remorse-filled that the Almighty chose her instead of me. She was the baby branch who withered first and abruptly from a tree of life, gone in too early a season.

There is one thing that I comprehend more now than ever before: once your purpose is fulfilled, no second chance is permissible. Her premonition of failing health was an inaudible voice surfacing to avert the uncoupling of another withering branch from our mother's rooted tree. My sister's descending health created a spirit of strangeness with a distance so far apart but a warning so close to sustain my motivation to solve the mystery of my mental illness.

The warning signs of my breakdown had theorized a strange malady interlinking cancer and mental illness. This was a caution commanding attention. A red alert was circulating, one sibling to the next.

Chapter 11

Sporting Mental Health Sanity

Mental illness is perhaps like sporting rivals competing to control or dominate an opponent by employing a psychological offense the other team is defenseless to defeat. Sports can be viewed as an entertaining distraction to an embattled life challenged by oppositional forces where losing is not an option. The conflict arises once an individual or even a team believes that the opponent is either far more aggressive or far less assertive. Neither was previously anticipated.

My spirited sport was not to throw, bounce, catch, or even kick a ball. Usually competition is between teams or individuals, but for me, it was between a friend and a foe. The enemy was mental illness, from which I was under constant attack by different symptoms and diagnoses. Some of the ailments were more determined to destroy me than others; it was like regular season games, divisional playoffs, and then conference championships.

The longer I fought, the more desperate the rivalry became, and the more my enemy resolved to end my season of life. My desire was to discover a sense of competition that ignited my will to fight this battle of life and death, with serious consequences for losing or winning. I began visualizing my mental illness as a competition, in which I was playing the most important game of all: the game of life. Competing subconsciously ignites a sense of determination, no matter one's age or gender. My willpower to win became more than just a game of quarters or endings. Conversely, my life had become an endurance sport in which I refuted that mental illness would be my finale, allowing my clock to run out of infinite time.

The essence of winning is instilled as early as childhood, when kids compete in Little League sports. Johnny is scolded by coaches, parents, and even teammates if Jane outperforms him. It is human nature to win and defeat the opponent, and we are oftentimes told in our everyday lives to outshine competitors in mostly everything we do. Winning makes the soul feel wholesome, but it can also establish a conceited level of superiority to be envied or esteemed.

Life will always have rivalries. I suppose it was comparable for me to assess that mental illness sometimes made me feel as though I was in a cutthroat competition between myself, my friends, and my foes, all aiming to destroy my sanity. Usually we hear people refer to adversarial opponents as haters, naysayers, or doubters. In my reality—although some perceived it as an illusion—I seemed to have all three. It was clear that someone had to win and someone had to lose, but it just could not be *me*.

I suppose one difference is that in sports, the beef is physically settled on the court or the field within a conclusive timeline. Meanwhile, for me, the mental illness sufferer, the beef was settled in my mental field of play, without a culminating timeline. I was experiencing multiple emotional adversaries that were competing to destroy my mind, requiring the expertise of a skilled coach. It was vital to revise and incorporate a new game plan daily to prevent competing illnesses from antagonizing me as an ill-prepared opponent. My sanity was not the only honor at stake, but also my legacy as a brave warrior and veteran, striving not to become a statistic.

As a sports fan, I have beheld the strange spirits of many people who influenced my journey toward recovery, and some may be hard to comprehend. Initially, I had dwindling faith as to whether I could manage or triumph over mental illness, because of my inner resistance. There were times when I lacked the will to fight; I had no inspiration or motivation to continue. Motivation is clearly necessary to inspire change on a personal level, but for some reason, I could not find a way to become motivated. This lack of motivation was enigmatic, because I was once a lively person who needed little motivation. I had been a successful warrior, a talented athlete, an excellent adult student, and, in a role that I was most proud of, a nurturing mother. These roles necessitated me to motivate not only my own children but my coworkers and teams.

Whenever people in my circle struggled to stay goal-oriented or adaptively in tune, I released a wand of inspiration. Ironically, I was the one needing to be magically motivated to refocus before taking another stride. I received motivation early in my career as a young soldier, but when I needed it most during my later career, it was either absent or a mystery. The one thing I know now is that when there is not a friend or foe to inspire you, there is always the favor of God.

My spiritual relationship has been challenged in so many instances throughout my life, causing me to wonder if I had not expected too much from God. Had I become opposed to utilizing the tools bestowed upon me? It was obvious as my struggles continued that I needed to activate those stricken talents lying deep within my flesh. It was not my character to succumb to anything. I had to compete instead of concede to an illness aiming to steal my quality of life.

Eventually, I realized that I yearned for a more forceful grit-and-grind mentality compelling me to seek something that would ignite a different level of motivation. To revolutionize one's mind-set, one must be exposed to a different setting, different people, or a different environment, asserting intervention by vision and then intuition. In other words, once you see differences, you begin to think differently. My mind had become sedentarily still, with inactivity restricting my capacity to think outside of my little box.

Suddenly one day, a breakthrough seemingly transpired as I was walking through my home of confining walls. The isolation felt so real, as if my ability to take the next step was halted on command.

I sensed that I had been locked away eternally—until I stumbled onto the living room floor. Was it accidentally or on purpose that I was guided into the living room, where I began to take a knee on the floor? This was the first time that I remember freely allowing myself to become vulnerable.

I began to acknowledge that I was wounded mentally, emotionally, and spiritually. Frankly, I had no other choice, because the walls within my life were becoming increasingly detached from reality. The reality of the outside world was no longer analogous to the inside world, where raging conflicts were constant. In other words, this type of shut-in existence had become my only source of relating.

As I lay on the floor, I sifted my surroundings from all the walls within the room, imagining what it would be like to extend my walls to new sites. Presently, those walls were untouchable, because my grasp was limited in this boxed containment without a window or a door. My life was so dark, and I just wanted a glimpse of light, with a new vision of roofless heights. I wanted to get another chance at life so that I could flourish with a new purposeful me.

In the past, I had purpose, both in my career and in my life as a mother and wife. The diagnosis of mental illness had stolen my purpose for living but also for being alive, trying to survive. GEMS gave me both purpose and support; however, it was never unconditional. It came with conditions that demanded my fateful submission, not my survival. I ached to break free from the mental suffocation of GEMS' control—to free my mind to return to the outside world unchained.

I lay on the floor staring up at the ceiling as if the roof would vanish, permitting my escape. Yet I mostly yearned for mental sovereignty, not necessarily physical exodus. I could exit the house at any time and yet be chained by my mental ineptness. I would lay on the floor for hours and hours each day, contemplating ways to take the first step toward self-recovery. The walls had no answers to offer, nor did the objects in the room appear talkative but mutely stared at me as if to say, "You, and only you, have the answers." In fact, GEMS was in the room as well, but I knew GEMS' time in my life was ending—or at least, that was my desire.

I communicated my desires in the open air and expressed aspirations that I desperately wanted for me and my family; however, I selfishly focused on me for a change. Undeniably, I was the main course, and no appetizer or dessert was desired on my plate, for it was already much too full. I was ready to gobble away all those unhealthy forethoughts that were bogging me down with extra mental mass. Believing a spiritual fast was within my reach, I prayed, meditated, cried, laughed, smiled, screamed, and even waddled around on the floor. My mind traveled in and out of multiple emotions, allowing my vulnerability to be celebrated instead of caged without any dominant emotion.

My receptiveness to my situation allowed my emotions to become free-flow, creating a fearless flourish. I began to feel winged and ready to fly away from a nested coop that was initially constructed for protection but had become one of confinement. I could feel in my spirit that a transformation was about to occur. Something or someone externally would have an unpredictable influence, awakening me to turn distress into defeat. Today was one of the first days in the past five years that I was dexterously equipped to be revived.

I was ready to rediscover life beyond the walls that I had inadvertently constructed with a willingness to deflect the effects of mental illness. The disparities encapsulating mental illness had become a part of who I was now, not necessarily who I was previously. The next few weeks were leading up to one of my most impactful appointments ever. Ironically, this doctor's assessment would be conducted in a different world, in a cagey location, because it was done through social media—specifically, Skype. I had not been aware of this type of medical care nor was I previously informed as to the situational backdrop of the appointment.

I still to this day believe it should be the patient's decision whether to interact in absence from the provider or face to face. Initially, I was not happy to discover the type of medical care I would be receiving and almost rescheduled the appointment. I became numb once I was told a Skype medical appointment had been chosen—of course, without input by or consideration for me. I felt medical Skype-ing lacked empathy for my situation but also the ability to relate emotionally to the expert providing the care. I was in for the surprise of my life.

I was escorted into a small office space, much like that closet setting where I previously communicated with GEMS. There were two chairs pushed to the back of a wall facing a thirty-two-inch television. Once I took one of the chairs to sit, an Arabic voice greeted me. "Hello, can you verify your name and date of birth?"

I complied, and the doctor proceeded to share his professional assessment regarding my health. He had an earful to share, and at the outset, I was unreceptive to what the doctor was imparting. It may have been because of his comments regarding my stylish appearance. Initially, I felt misjudged. He may have meant it as a compliment, but I took it as a criticism—as if ill people should not be well-groomed.

Oftentimes, people perceive your physical appearance to be a reflection of your mental state, not realizing that those seemingly harmless comments can be seen as insolent. It is rare that an ill person is externally and internally the same. That would be sci-fi itself, to be able to diagnose an individual by sight rather than by symptoms. So, I thought, should I not comb my hair, bathe, make up my face, dress well, or act civilized? That phrase, "You don't look like anything is wrong," is so hollow. Such comments often made me feel like someone was second-guessing my diagnosis. Perhaps nothing was wrong, and maybe I was restored. Contradicting my feelings, my emotions, and my senses in this way only delayed my recovery.

The doctor conversed with me for about forty-five minutes, and although it seemed as if we were getting nowhere, we did indeed go somewhere—to a place only a spiritual being could relate to. Let's hit the pause button, because this doctor's appointment was not conducted at a church or a mosque but at a military health facility. The doctor was a civilian employed by the Veterans Administration to care for retired, reservist, and some active-duty soldiers. I never consulted or previously was a patient of this doctor. The military appointment database usually assigns medical providers with limited input if any from the veteran.

This appointment from the beginning was strange, but as the minutes passed, it became even more curious. The doctor shared that he believed in me and that I had the fuel to ignite my own recovery, but I would have to magnify my spiritual faith. This may not sound like a typical suggestion from a typical doctor, but this journey of recovery has been nothing but atypical. Without hesitating, he told me that my journey would require a strong relationship with God so that I could redeem my health—mentally, emotionally, and most important, spiritually.

I believe he was like an angel, offering mental clarity that motivated me to seek spiritual recovery. Oh my, his words were like music to my ears. Two weeks' earlier, all I did was meditate and pray to God. I cried out for his mercies upon my life and health. This was not only a blessing but a confirmation that I was on my way to recovery.

I am not saying that I was freed of any mental illness or disorder, but I was freed from the chains that enclosed my mind and forced me to surrender to a demonic power. This is not about whether mental illness is devilish or a demon, but it unveils an unknown supremacy that was seeking my demise. This appointment was undoubtedly beneficial, but its purpose was not to persuade me to ignore my traditional treatments. Instead, it encouraged me to intensify my faith and believe that I could recover.

Recovery has a multitude of contexts, which reassured me that I was covered with the blood of the lamb, not the curse of the enemy. I had several nemeses that had antagonized my spirits from within my soul. These nemeses were causing me to disavow my willpower to recover as an absent *self* instead of a present *me*. Mental illness can become affectively uncontrollable, just like an untreated winter cold, without proper treatment or therapies. It has the tendency to transgress into something more worrisome, with layers of distress.

However, mental illness is a different species that imposes a far greater emotional detriment than the flu, which has symptomatic remedies. Mental illness often involves dormant effects that lie in remission until the mind becomes exposed to signs of emotional infiltration involving an illness, injury, or traumatic incident.

I believe that my mental illness and disorders ascended based upon an array of traumatic incidents. Injuries can inflict emotional wounds, triggering the mind to lapse or perhaps pause—as I experienced—in its ability to function. I grappled with the fact that being diagnosed with mental illness did not insinuate that I had become a cracked box but rather that there were hidden cracks within the walls that required a timely restoration. Since my diagnosis, I occasionally speculate about other people's mental illnesses. I imagine them being like me, raided by invasive mental illnesses that stifle their quality of life.

This speculation led me to contemplate realities for victims who suffer from other traumas, like rape, shootings, life-threatening illnesses, unexpected losses, divorce, or physical injuries that too can impact one's mentality. Comparing these traumatic struggles allowed me to further comprehend that I am no different from those who suffer from other emotionally or mentally draining injuries. Coincidentally, I just had an injury that is often perceived with heightened misconceptions: that a person suffering from mental illness is unhinged or to be feared. Again, I am neither, so I had to discover someone to motivate me but also something inspirational and entertaining.

It had to be an activity that took me mentally away from my existing circumstances while helping me face my condition in a different mood of fulfillment. The one thing that kept me moving was sports. I was very active as a teen and enjoyed basketball and track. One of my high school coaches tried to lure me into playing tennis, but that was never an aspiration. I always had a competitive spirit for winning, however, and now that I had children, I encouraged them to partake in sports as well.

My son, Jostein, was becoming a thriving athlete. His sporting events as a young adolescent kept me intrigued and excited about sports from the start of Little League. Attending Jostein's basketball and football events was prideful; I believed he had great potential and that he got his athletic talent from me. Of course, I would never tell his father that Jostein's genetic traits were rooted by me and not him. That is funny, and surely my husband would agree, but for a different reason. He was only a participant in youth sports and not quite as ambitious about competition—but certainly he never wanted to lose. I hoped Jostein would one day seek the next level of competitiveness.

I enjoyed multiple sport activities, but football and basketball were my favorites. An occupation that consistently requires such a high level of competitiveness must be mentally and emotionally draining. The expectations of competition, injury risks, traveling, extensive scheduling, franchise demands, fans, and above all the need to win is exhausting just thinking about it. It may seem that it is all fun, with lots of money, but even with all the perks, I believe the physical wear and tear puts one in jeopardy to fall even when they appear to be standing.

In high school, during a basketball district playoff game, I suffered a knee injury. I went to the emergency room, and the physician told me that my season was over based upon my injury. I was not only stunned but felt subconsciously that there was no way I could not play. It was my junior year, with a chance to win a championship. My mind, for some reason, took sole ownership of everything my body was incapable of doing. My mind became overburdened with the what-ifs, whys, would-of-could-of-should-ofs.

Frankly, I was overwhelmingly depressed and fearful as to what was going to happen regarding not only if I could play the next game but also what if never again? The divergences between physical and mental injuries presented a frontal disparity in detecting an obscure versus an obvious symptomatic sign of injury. A physical injury permits immediate discovery, whereas mental injuries go habitually unnoticed, hiding signs of injurious effects to the mind. The norm in our society is to examine what we see, not what we cannot see. This leaves wounds to fester, causing unforeseen detriments.

Although I played different sports throughout my adolescent, I had no idea of the importance of diffusing past sports ambitions in my future sports admiration. Initially, I did not know where to begin at connecting the dots, until suddenly it struck me while watching an NBA game. I began to contemplate the resiliency of injured NBA players and how an injury could impact their will to overcome adversity from both a physical and mental standpoint. I cannot but surmise that it is a struggle that many players will not openly admit to for fear of the backlash of perception but also the backdrop to the legacy of their careers.

This is a situation that many owners, teams, coaches, players, and families give little thought to because the injury is one of concealment. I began to analyze my theory more closely when some of my favorite NBA players suffered injuries. Incredibly, there were two NBA players who impacted my mental illness recovery in a way I never imagined. They both suffered sport injuries, causing them to be sidelined by unforeseen incidents while playing the game they loved to play and I loved to watch.

My basketball hobby started in high school, where I learned to be a two-way threat, possessing more defensive skill than offensive skills. I was a defensive player who was always seen as a relentless piece of armor, suffocating opposing elite players with a relentless attack. I became a fan of one of the NBA's most well-skilled teams in the Western conference. I was no doubt their biggest supporter and oftentimes envisioned myself as a mom-fan. I would not only root and cheer for them, but I had no problem scolding them while screaming at the television as they went up and down the court. Comically, I would laugh after yelling, realizing they could not hear me, but in spirit I was so connected. It was if I was a lion rooting for her cubs to do their very best: win!

There were two NBA stars I relished to see play for a long, long time, and I imagined that one day that dream would come true. They both were competitively ruthless, demonstrating such a driven spirit to cope with adversity caused by on-the-court injuries. These two one-of-a-kind athletes suffered unthinkable injuries, but their determination sparked new life into my aspiration to overcome my own illness.

Many people believe an injury is an injury, but I assure you, it differs based on the individual and the injury. Recovery is an expectation of every person who suffers an injury. However, there are no guarantees, which makes the latter feat so important. It is the will of the fighter to recuperate. Most people will experience some type of an injury throughout their lives, but it is how you bounce back after taking the fall that counts.

I felt like an athlete undergoing physical retrogression that sometimes caused me to wonder whether I would ever fully recover—presumably, like athletes who suffer injuries. I suppose it is the creeping doubt of uncertainty that causes people to succumb to the ill fate of psychological fear. I was always told that it's mind over matter if you want to triumph over any obstacle. As a warrior, I believe this veracity from within the depths of my core.

There are many athletes who closed-mindedly deal with some type of mental illness that may not be caused by an injury but rather the pressures of the league's expectations. Depression, anxiety, and other illnesses can arise, whether for athlete or avid fans. The fear for most is being ostracized and labeled crazy—something I am all too familiar with but certainly not a fan of. It is an unfair expectation to claim that an injury cannot impact an individual's mental stability. No matter how strong or courageous an individual appears on the surface as a competitor, mental illness is one of the most relentless opponents imaginable.

I yearned to conceptually collaborate with an idolizing team or group of competitors that could uplift my spirits. These two players motivated me so much after seeing them return to their livelihood as athletes after suffering severe, unpredictable, sidelining injuries. The injuries instigated a temporary hiatus during the season, and many believed altered the possibility of making a deep run in the playoffs. I had rarely missed any games in the past five years, no matter where I was or what I was doing. I was in-synch with the NBA game schedules, ensuring I did not miss any desired games. In fact, everything was on pause whenever the television was focused on teams and players that I delighted to watch.

Whenever I watched specific players, it was like an antidote to my soul and therapy for my recovery. I had gone through so much that cheering for a team of megastars allotted a tangible vision where I could socially integrate. It reminded me of my military service, where being part of a team was amazingly fulfilling in an unfathomable way. After twenty-two years of military service, it has been challenging to replace that bond of sisterhood or brotherhood working for a commonality to achieve a bilateral goal. The military signifies a traditional paradigm of teamwork, yielding a lifelong camaraderie much like sports teams, especially those that established championship relationships. I still desire that level of camaraderie, even though I have since retired.

I shared my emotional and mental struggles throughout my intimate encounter with mental illness, but I became curious as to whether an athlete who suffers an injury also struggles to recover. I recall watching one of my favorite players suffer a knee injury during a game of two Western conference NBA teams. I thought for a second that the physical contact causing the injury would not result in an off-the-court medical assessment. However, suddenly, I like other fans watched his fate turn into fear as he exited the floor. Coincidentally, another of my favorite basketball stars was sidelined with the possibility of a career-ending injury. I am sure many were frightened that he would not have the durability to return because of the state of his physique. I never doubted either of their recoveries, even though I was looking from the outside in.

We fanatics sometimes have the audacity to express unsolicited opinions not because we know the truths but because we want to predict uncertain outcomes. Some of us are so invested that we lose sight of the fact that these personal circumstances do not directly involve or affect us. We are just living vicariously through those we idolize and admire. I was confident that each of them would recover physically but perhaps struggle with other uncertainties. As a former athlete, I can attest that it takes an internal drive to repair, rebuild, and recondition the body to its previous state after a major injury. Honestly, not all can undergo or endure the same impact, whether a mental or physical injurious setback.

It is assumed that it's mind over matter and not the reverse, since the mind is the controlling entity of responsive reflection. Some outsiders may ask, "What does sports have to do with mental illness recovery?" I suppose it is not unusual to believe that corresponding parallels exist, with associative linkage between an injury and the mind. Some but not all injuries can induce some type of anxiety or fear that initiates emotional doubt or mental despair. I believe someone who is impacted by a major injury has at one point contemplated how the injury may affect overall health, which can become burdensome to the mind.

There are so many pressures to recover, but as well expectations to perform as before the injury, especially for players in the NBA, NFL, MLB, and other sports. As a soldier, I felt the pressures, which led to my early retirement. I struggled with the expectations to recover—even though there were medical professionals who doubted that I could. Just imagine that! The career fulfillment of your dreams is jeopardized by an inadvertent incidence of injury. An injury can occur to anyone, at any time, for reasons unforeseen.

I am not claiming that either of these amazing athletes suffered from mental illness in any type of way, but there exists data that some do. I am perhaps concluding that no matter who you are, if an unexpected injury, illness, or trauma interrupts your livelihood, it can lead to indefinite levels of mental despair. If athletes were candid regarding the psychological injuries of hidden scars, most of them might acknowledge that despondency surrounding mental emotions is undeniable pressuring, although some might attempt to refute this notion.

People suffering from an illness or injury may also attest that recovery is dependent upon the elasticity of each injured person.

Usually, people become motivated by different aspirations in life. For me, it appeared to be a forum of competition. Luckily for me, connecting with my favorite two NBA stars aided tremendously during my recovery. It was like witnessing resiliency from afar, where these athletic idols fought to return from dark uncertainty to a promising spotlight. For five years, I watched and dreamed of seeing them play in person and hoped one day it would come true. I wanted not only to attend a game but to be up close and personal so that I could let them know the inspiration they provided to me during my recovery. Sometimes it is hard for even me to comprehend their impact, so for anyone reading, please do not even try, because it is too mystical.

My goal was to do everything possible to meet at least one of them if not both. My recovery was already underway, but my desire was to share my journey and express their impact to strangers and fans. I told my husband that I desperately wanted to see them play in person. The mere fact that my husband and I both are retired veterans makes attending an NBA game for a family of five far too expensive, especially for front-row seats. Still, I told my husband that all I wanted to do for my forty-seventh birthday was attend one of their games, and it would be amazing to see the team play against a rival team, simply because I root for competitiveness at its heights, not its depths. I enjoy NBA players who grind and compete, displaying their phenomenal talents, which are truly a blessing, requiring unparalleled work ethic.

My husband and I researched tickets at different locations and quickly realized that with consideration to our other obligations, it was just not within reach. Nevertheless, I never give up on something I wanted, nor did I allow any circumstance to avert the aspirations I hungered for the most. My family made an unbelievable sacrifice for me to see my favorite two players when they visited the Dallas Mavericks in February, 2016. This was the most amazing birthday gift ever—even though it was a belated gift. The atmosphere was electrifying! I did not get front row seats, but I was close enough to gaze from afar with nothing but excitement.

I yelled and screamed both players' names, but of course they are so accustomed to seeing and hearing fans that my voice was only a floating vapor in the cheering air. I had one request for my family, since this was a breathtaking dream come true. I wanted to savor the moment. I required everyone in our family to wear the gear of my favorite two players. It wasn't too difficult to persuade them, because my son and I favored one of the same players. My son reminds me of them both, while his chosen is opposite of mine. He wore a jersey without a number to give homage to them both.

He's built like one of my favorites with a great outside shot, but his aggression is relentless like the other; he's not afraid to attack as a guard. If they were to ever become aware of how impactful their tenacity has been for me, it would be humbling to meet them, although they are no longer on the same team. I must admit that watching them play a game on television is far different from watching them play in person. Witnessing their talent in real life made an illusory vision a palpable reality, transcending a personal yet heartfelt story. The relevance I imagined was an amazing impact made by a stranger I knew only from afar, but who I felt like I knew more closely.

I am forever a fan of the game, but even more so continue to be a fan of the Oklahoma City Thunder and Russell Westbrook. I just had to see another game in person, so for my forty-eighth birthday, I got tickets to see the Thunder play in Dallas. I was assured weeks in advance by a family liaison of the Dallas Mavericks that they would arrange for me to meet Russell Westbrook after the game. I was tickled with polka dots, not pink, because my thoughts were dotted with different emotions. Weeks and days went by, and I became more anxious with each passing hour to meet Westbrook. Everyone in my circle knew it. I would even share that I could not stop chattering about this possibility!

It was finally here: the game where the Oklahoma Thunder was scheduled to play the Dallas Mavericks. My family was fortunate to purchase tickets months in advance. The tickets were bought as a dual gift—Christmas and birthday—which made them extremely special for all of us. It was a cloudy day, but no rain could spoil my sunshine on this day. It was a Sunday game, so we did not have to worry about a workday for my husband, and for my children, it was spring break beginning that Monday. We arrived to the game early so we could pick up the passes to meet Russell Westbrook after the game.

We proceeded to the "Will Call" ticketing area to retrieve the passes so that we could remain in the arena after the game. No passes were there on our first two attempts, but on the third attempt, the passes were ready for pickup. I was little skeptical at this point but remained somewhat optimistic; after all, I had waited almost three years or more.

The game did not go well for the Thunder. We lost that night, 109 to 98, which was disappointing. Westbrook was such a competitor that he took the loss personally, retreating to the locker room. I understood that, because most high-performing competitors always want to win and impact the game. After the game, I proceeded to the area where fans got an opportunity to meet and be greeted by players. I was so excited!

There were about fifty people staged in an area after the game, and my heart was thumping so hard, like a loud time-clock buzzer. About fifteen or twenty minutes passed, and suddenly some of the Thunder players ascended from the locker room. The first couple of players that emerged were Andre Roberson, Domantas Sabonis, Doug McDermott, Semaj Christon, and Nick Collison but no Russell Westbrook. I began to think Westbrook was not going to come out of the locker room, especially since the team lost and it being a road game.

We waited about ten minutes more, and still no Westbrook. Abruptly, a brown-skinned man appeared in front of me as I was standing in the nearby designated seating. He subtly spoke to some family members and said, "He's not coming out of the locker room."

I did not know who the gentleman was, but I was curious. I asked my husband to ask the man whether he was related to Westbrook. The man resembled him and looked very familiar.

My husband said, "Excuse me, are you Westbrook's dad?"

The man was quite humble and replied, "Yes, I am Westbrook's dad!"

My husband spoke briefly with Westbrook's father as they embraced each other with a man-hug. My husband introduced Mr. Westbrook to me, and he shook my hand. I briefly shared with him the inspirational impact his son had during my mental illness struggle and recovery. I also told him that I would appreciate it if he told his son. He thanked me on behalf of his son, and we took a picture together. Unfortunately, two birthdays and a book later, I still have not met Westbrook, but I remain optimistic. I am glad that at least I met the father of one of the most entertainingly skilled basketball players ever to play the game.

I watched Kevin Durant and Russell Westbrook play the game in person, and it seemed as if they'd never suffered an injury, dominating the game just as well or even better than before. Westbrook's recovery seems matchless in comparison to others who have struggled to return. This athlete is something special! I recall some of the verbal adversities he underwent a few years earlier, where naysayers fouled his soul game after game, but now we are thunderstruck as groupies boast about and extol his talents. Nonetheless, Westbrook has become so relevant to the game that those once-relevant metaphors have now become irrelevant scrutiny, fulminating his skills no matter fan or foe.

I am forever a fan of the game, the Thunder, and certainly Westbrook. His consistency to be incomparable no matter the adversity or obstacle underscores his position as a player, teammate, and role model. He is a positive representation of strength of mind and will to fight and never give in to what "they" say—do *you* not *they*.

It is necessary to advocate for those who undergo medical triumphs in life—especially an illness or injury that can lead to debilitation of not only the body but also the mind. It became clear that intrinsic recovery was the most obvious depiction of immeasurable progression. Recovery can be witnessed by the eye, but the depths it impacts lie beneath an individual's spirit. My motivation has grown exponentially over the past five years, allowing me to confront hidden anxieties and fears head on. I thank those who have inspired me, even if I never make a personal connection.

Chapter 12

Strangers' Face-to-Face Confrontation

It was time to confront this demonic stranger, but was I ready? Facing adversity is never easy, but it was necessary to advance my steps forward regardless of certainty or uncertainty. The map to my recovery was no longer encrypted with foreign lingo. The therapies fluctuated in the context of permanency versus impermanency, which prompted me to navigate an altered route to a more mystical destination.

These fluctuating routes often blocked my mental ability to interpret whether I was traveling north or south. Progress was to move north, and regression meant I was falling backward to a southern demise. I witnessed other people prevail past adversities where crossroads intersected and interchanged. Finally, it was my chance to take control as the navigator controlling my destination. It was time to execute a U-turn onto a new road that could have been viewed as prohibited by some; however, for me it was permitted.

I was not afraid of breaking any laws. I had been imprisoned far too long. I yearned for freedom, no matter the charge. Perhaps my doctor assumed I was speeding; therefore, he prescribed additional therapies of treatment. One of the treatments sent shock waves through my feeble body, soul, and mind.

One of my health providers decided to prescribe a specific type and dosage to promote a healthier balance for managing my mental and emotional stability. I was doing well, but based upon some of my shifting symptoms, a higher dosage was advised. Although I was skeptical, I complied to avoid refuting the professional's directives. My goal was to ensure that I was receptive to anything to improve my chances for a healthier life for me and my family.

Initially, I felt as if I had no right to reject any professional recommendation aimed at making me better. I should have at least gotten a second opinion, because some choices are not retractable, especially those that are health-driven. I endorsed the dosage change without a thorough vetting of the decision. Sometimes there's a change without a screening of the details. I was perplexed as to the reason for making changes to my medical plan regarding medication consumption versus cognitive therapeutics.

I preferred not to ingest medication as a quick fix, especially prescriptions meant to palliate symptoms surrounding mental illness. During my esophagus intake, the medications seemed to impose an immediate but residual affect that factually left me speechless. I was wordless because of the incapacitation of not knowing who I was or comprehending the powerful spellbinding hypnosis absorbing my presence. I felt absent while present in another molding.

During my mental illness antics, there were a multitude of medicines prescribed by numerous doctors, searching to discover measurable remedies to treat my symptoms. Dialogue between patient and doctor is critical pertaining to prescribing specific medications. Medications are consumed to treat the patient but can also cause varying side effects from one patient to the next. Patient vigilance to detect reactionary change or response can weigh heavily in deciding whether the pros or cons are beneficial to health. Sometimes the side effects of the medications outweigh the risks, and there are times that risks are far too great without being beneficial.

I ingested a new medication that was prescribed by a provider. I had never ingested anything that made me plead for relief. My body ached for six hours, causing an unusual response that seemed to reject the pills I consumed. The medications were taken to promote cerebral balance in calming my emotions. In fact, they did the very opposite, demoting my therapeutic progress and mounting my emotive fears.

The ingestion made me drift away into midair like I was a withered leaf. I immediately lost control in a multiplex mode, leading to weakened limbs. Suddenly, I collapsed to the floor, falling into my husband's arms. I started vomiting everywhere: all over myself, the floor, and the furniture. This volcanic release went on for three hours, creating a mystery for both me and Budd. I vomited on Budd at least ten times. This would have frustrated most people, but not my Budd. He remained calm, trying to comfort me and console my fears.

This was a horrible scene, a room filled with disgust and physical woes that was at the same time saturated with an unbelievable display of compassion. Budd not once left my side as he struggled to figure out why this medication did so much to me so quickly in such a devilish outpour. Some may suggest there was possibly an allergic reaction, but it was not my first time consuming this medication. I had been prescribed the medication in the past but was inconsistent in consuming it on a regular basis. I believe the dosage had slightly changed as well.

At any rate, an allergic reaction was not what I felt symptomatically. There was no rash, burning sensation, or fever, but instead something clashing within my spirit. I felt like a possessed spirit had invaded my body, and something was being sputtered out like a combustible explosion. It was clear that I had ingested something that was either much too potent or ignited the release of something that did not belong. Either way, my organic system had immediately become intolerable, strong-arming me to cramp as I moaned louder and louder. Budd and I struggled to relieve my aching misery.

I felt helpless in the face of this unknown, coercive power embedded in my belly. We could see the movement of my abdomen as waves of skin moved upward and downward. The only thing to left to contemplate was, what is going on? Budd carried me to our bedroom and laid me flat onto the bed so he could visualize the movement more clearly. He rubbed and massaged my stomach to relieve the cramping.

It was as if I was birthing something strange—perhaps a new me. There was clearly some sort of metamorphosis taking place, a purging of my debility from within. My body was being purged of infections like a detoxification or cleansing. This process was ignited by the exact medication that was prescribed to stabilize my mood but at this point was executing a more profound decontamination. I suppose I was being ridded of complex ailments that would lead to the release of emotive detriments with renewal of a sensitive disposition.

I was changing and feeling transformed and wholesome, with newly implanted emotions that I did not previously sense, but the presence of change was seen. I was prescribed different medications by multiple doctors, which is mind-blowing. These professionals were either psychiatrists or psychologists as well a neurologist. I was supposed to become better by self-medicating myself to treat these ailments. In the past, I tried to comply with the doctors' directives, always taking my prescriptions, but I always felt zombielike.

The compilation of my prescribed medications created a numbness with an oblivion to even know myself or my surroundings. Some of the medications I was simultaneously prescribed were Maxalt-LT, Topermax, Lamictal, Effexor XR, Silenor, and Abilify. I was even prescribed Prozac, which presented side effects that made me very weary of my state of mind. Medications are meant to heal the body but can sometimes hinder the body's innate recovery depending on the ailment or injury. I am not bashing any provider who prescribes meds to mental illness sufferers. However, not all medications can treat all persons, because not all mental illnesses are the same.

I found it unusual that most of my peer sufferers, while assigned to the mental hospital, were prescribed the same medication as I was, even though our visible symptoms appeared so unalike. I strongly believe different rehabilitations are critical in determining what is best for the patient by ensuring proper dosage of medications, therapies, and support systems to aid in recovery. I felt as though people like me suffering from mental illness are oftentimes prescribed specific medications as a quick fix, with no consideration of the long-term impact to our health recovery. I was afraid of being overly medicated, which may have induced an inadvertent addiction to prescription drugs. This was the reason I chose to either not ingest some of the medications, intake a minimal dosage, or ensure infrequent consumption.

Everyone has different emotions and motives that drive their transformation to recovery. However, not everyone is stable enough to detect the awkwardness as to how some therapies can be rejected internally as well as externally when the body refuses to concur with certain treatments, especially prescriptions. Mental illness is such a volatile struggle, putting the mind on a roller coaster ride. The ride is unsettling, with constant fears if no deliberate controls exist to redirect movement with resolution.

I became dazed, bilious, and unsteady, and I experienced brief detachments. My brain began to fail in transmitting one movement to the next with a sensory responsiveness. Since being diagnosed, I often wondered how or why some sufferers struggle more than others or why some act out in ways that others do not. Particularly, I wondered why some sufferers commit unthinkable offenses against innocent people that are known violations. I believe it has something to do with the mind's inability to respond to or reject the notion of what is wrong or right at any given time.

Access to treatment and early detection is critical in diagnosing injured minds. It is unquestionable that lacking a way to gain access to mental illness health care can create a stagnancy for cure and recovery. In the past, our communities have witnessed the devastation and havoc caused by someone experiencing mental struggles. In my opinion, it can inadvertently lead to a level of insanity because of disparaging treatment in an exclusive world versus an inclusive environment.

People act out in different ways, times, and circumstances. Repeatedly after tragedy strikes, it becomes more evident that the risks surrounding mental illness can impact others just as much as the sufferer. We become alarmed as a society but continue rejecting any notion that mental illness is real and that treatment is a necessity. The responses to these cries for help usually display insignificant empathy, with provisional acts of concern. These silent cries are becoming more detrimental, and if society keeps failing to acknowledge them, the sounding responses will become more roused.

Mental illness was a coercive antagonist that made me feel, without warning, shunned by society, my loved ones, and even my community. I am unsure whether my emotions were publicly detectable, but for certain some were viewed with suspicion. I may not have felt shunned if openness was an option, but there never seemed to be an alternative to remaining encaged. It is imperative for sufferers like me to have an accessible gateway to therapies that LAST: love, acknowledgement, support, and time. This bridging of empathetic words entered my psyche, creating a heightened desperation for hope rather than unending despair. Once I realized different resources were needed to supplement my support, I began to feel more empowered. It was not until years later—after my diagnosis, a change of environment, and quality time with loved ones—that my life began to progress.

There were times when I suffered from issues that were rampant in my earlier state of mind versus things happening in an existing state of mind. I felt as though I was present in a physical sense but absent by withdrawal, coexisting in a nonexistent state in relation to my actions. There were incidents where I experienced rage or anger that led to outbursts, excessive yelling, screaming, and sometimes profane language. I realized it was me acting out, but then again, I was an incoherent body, riddled by the effects of an illness that was pressurizing my reactions. The pressures of emotional combustion became unbearable, all because I felt mentally and emotionally captive, without any form of freedom with the exception of my words.

I never wanted to lash out physically during my mental illness struggles; however, I recall my therapist and psychologist inquiring as to that possibility on numerous occasions: "Are you suicidal or homicidal?" Honestly, I am not sure who would answer yes, but of course, I imagine some would. I believe that clear hints are left by those who feel suicidal or homicidal as a last cry to be saved from others as well themselves. At this point, the individual is in complete despair, without any hope. However, when I found myself at the point of suicide, I chose not to utter a word. Silence became a danger for me while suffering from mental illness. Once I withdrew, that was perhaps the most alarming sign.

I just found the question to be too forthright, because as a sufferer, my desire was to continuously evade directness. I also avoided providing too much insight as to my intentions while barricaded within my own cells of solitude. I believe the probe should be couched differently to solicit feedback rather than to invite an immediate closed-ended response. Although you are comfortably couched with plush seating, there is very little plushness in addressing issues that are so isolating. "Yes" and "no" are just too blunt—an easy way out of a difficult engagement to confront one's intentions. For me, a more open-ended question may have caused a break: "If you were suicidal, how would you commit suicide?" If anyone has contemplated suicide, the details would most likely be very descriptive rather than imaginative.

During the past several years, our society has dealt with emotional outbursts from people who appear normal, sound, and even socially integrated. However, we do not need to ignore the presence of questionable incidents that possibly illustrate some type of mental illness. I remember being called into an office to be scolded by a team of superiors. These superiors displayed a level of censure after I repudiated compliance regarding a deeply personal issue over which their decision was too partial. Somehow, they assumed based upon their positions of authority, I would cowed by their blatant disregard for me and my family.

I had recently returned from Iraq and had only been in association with this leadership for about four months. I was struggling to reintegrate with these inexperienced, non-deployed leaders who offered no empathy. I did not disobey any laws or policies warranting any Uniform Code of Military Justice (UCMJ) actions. However, I requested a meeting to express my disappointment as to the exerting of command authority involving an upsetting family matter. At this point, I had not been diagnosed with any mental illness, nor am I certain it existed. Nevertheless, based upon this interaction with my superiors, unfamiliar behavior was evidently on display, revealing a different canvas with an overcast of shades.

I believe mental illness is filled with changing shades of colorlessness that suggests that it is not the color that one sees but the color that one senses. It is like a mixture of paints with the inability to detect any potency using the naked eye, whether by conception or prevalence. One or the other can become more dominant depending on the angle of view, which can sometimes alter.

Presumably, most everyone of a certain age, beginning at adolescence and into adulthood, has taken an eye exam. Eye exams usually require medical assessment amid repressed hue colors, signaling if any issues are hidden, lying dormant from external detection. The eyes glare frontally, even though within view it is difficult to pinpoint the location of the hidden object. As one wearily gazes, suddenly an impression appears, and you wonder, *What took so long? It's right in my face!* The angle and concentration of detectability is vaguely inconclusive, especially when one is blinded by mystery.

Mental illness and disorders are parallels of cryptic emotions that change one's feelings into one's reaction. It even looks abstruse from a different angle, requiring committed vigilance to diagnose from afar as well up close, where the proximity of sight can become divergent. No one can say unequivocally what mental illness looks like, but perhaps many can share what it feels like. Therefore, if society promotes advocacy for mental illness, it perhaps can be detected sooner rather than later.

It's easy to say, "Mental illness doesn't look like me." It looks more fictional than tangible because of tainted societal misconceptions. Please do not allow yourselves to be misled by the infestation of such an enervating yet suffocating disease as mental illness. Far too often, society displays sorrowfulness after a crisis, which is so humanly disingenuous. The most hypocritical pretense is that society pants only for a moment without any action, where time after time individuals surrender as prey to mental illness.

The impact of feeling emotionally denigrated and perceptibly disregarded by my previous superiors had lasting implications that I never considered until after undergoing intense therapies. I discovered just how much rage was deeply secreted within my cerebral core, surrounding the devastating decisions my superiors attempted, aiming to impose overt career impediments. There was an occurrence prior to my diagnosis after returning from the war when I contemplated committing an act of homicide. I wanted to cause injury to people in my workplace because of the emotional detriment they were inflicting without remorse or inclination of harm to my family. I am not a violent-tempered person or warrior, but I am very candidly open. I factually knew of a group of people were purposefully aiming to destroy my career and livelihood by demonstrating manipulative power. It was humiliating, and it angered me to the depths of my soul that people would take a personal concern and transpose it to a professional conflict, all for the sake of being in power.

It started with a crisis surrounding the health of my spouse, not myself. We had sacrificed so much, and at this exact time, little empathy was displayed to aid us with reintegration into a life of normalcy after the Iraqi war. It was as if the enemy was confronting me on my own turf with friendly fire. This was not supposed to occur, nor was it expected. I contemplated revenge in a myriad of ways, imagining myself confronting my home-turf enemies with not just words but actions. I wanted to inflict pain and make them feel what I was feeling. The only difference was that my pain was mental and emotional, while I believe theirs was contentious because of a position of superiority. At the time, I believed the only way to get even was to inflict harm that was substantially felt.

Decisions were being made that were not only cruel and inhumane but also possessing a hidden agenda that was soon revealed at the core of these persons' covert intent. Sometimes it may be hard to know what ignites struggles of the mind, which may be some unknown villain. I earlier conveyed the possibility of an injury, illness, and genetic infiltrations, but incidents of toxic detriment can introduce another variable. Antagonistically, it could very well be the will of the people you surround yourself with who overtly divert your path.

The people in my work circle of authority congested my mental space with the constancy of their injurious decisions. This lasted for about fourteen months, causing me to believe I was temporarily stupid but abidingly smart. I sat in my car day in and day out trying to figure out a way to disband myself from this hostile situation, dodging the expense of my liberty. Have you ever had someone so powerfully influential and controlling that they deliberately dangled your livelihood so boldly in your presence—frankly, to the point where they assumed there was nothing you could do about it? This was one of those instances, but they underestimated the resilient willpower of a warrior.

I could not believe the crooked deviousness being done to eradicate my twelve-year career. It was if I was inconsequential, although impacted by the consequences of leadership's decisions as they conspired to ensure that I was seen as ash without a trace of professional DNA. The fact that I worked hard, followed the rules, and produced measurable results was irrelevant.

After my expression of disagreement, a battle ensued. I thought I was senseless and had committed a crime against the world, or perhaps my leadership. My mind played tricks on me from time to time, causing me to feel guilt, but it was just plain delusional that I was the culpable party. I was not about to allow myself to be foolishly ill-treated when in fact it was not my battle, it was theirs. I just needed to prove it.

I fought relentlessly, abstaining from making one of the worst mistakes of my life, one that might have led to my death or incarceration. I was determined and motivated to win this battle. I finally obtained a change in career venue with the support of a highly esteemed general officer who endorsed my unrelenting efforts to be the victor, not the victim. This general's endorsement led to a job promotion of five ranks higher, with a significant increase in salary.

My mental illness was a testament to my mind's tenacity to unpredictably travel from one place to another, resetting into a state of predictable stabilities. After traveling back and forth during various episodes of detriment, I sensed it was time to embark on a more directional journey. It was time to say farewell to another foe in my life, as I had done a time or two in the past. Saying farewell is never easy, but it was very necessary to rid people, ailments, infirmities, or weaknesses from my life.

The battle to overcome my mental illness adversity was one of the most tumultuous adventures in my life. After miles of wear and tear on my body, mind, and soul, I was awakened from a mass of stillborn ailments. The pain that I felt during the ingestion of prescribed remedies had aided in aborting complex symptoms of mental illness from within the pits of my core. Thereafter, I began experiencing new sights, sounds, and silences through which I navigated on a journey toward unfamiliar roads and bridges. These new pathways reconnected my thoughts while unlocking belted phobias, allowing me to rediscover myself.

Chapter 13

Farewell My Beloved, GEMS

T he fabric of who you are can be de-quilted by the hands of another if and only if you allow yourself to be patched in pieces instead of sewn with permanence. Nonetheless, somehow, I was unable to pinpoint the evolution of my demise once I began suffering from rupturing emotions. These unstable emotions had inadvertently breached the normalcy of my sound behaviors, causing unconscious stillness. My mind acted as though it was splintered into shattered fragments that triggered a sudden breakaway from life. The rupturing of my thoughts in some eeriness allowed my mental illness to become a passing wound, but for many the wound is permanent. However, I was on a mission to heal and restore my being by confronting GEMS face to face—even if it meant loss of life—to salvage myself.

Do you remember that initial party invitation you assented to as my VIP guests? Well, every host should extend graciousness, so I am honored that you obliged my request to attend this revelry. Please stand and applaud my closing moments as I say farewell to my beloved GEMS. GEMS and I met during a time of wrath-filled darkness, spanning over five turbulent years. It would be dismissive of me as a host if I did not express the same to you as VIPs for joining me. This has been a battle from within, clashing with a ferocious stranger. This foe-stranger was winning for many years while I was losing this ongoing battle. I won the war, but this fight was not only difficult but contentious for me as well as other mental illness sufferers. Nevertheless, this love affair is over, and sharing my farewell to GEMS was critical in advancing my steps toward recovery.

GEMS had become consciously implanted as a domineering part of my cerebrum, growing unrestrained stems of uncertainty. I could no longer be of two minds with one mission, so it was necessary that I revert into my own existence without this powerful impairment. GEMS' was a love that suffocated my emotions and comprehension while inducing fears and anxieties that made me lose when all I wanted to do was win. I met GEMS in a different closet in Texas, and now it would be impossible to return to that same old closet since my unexpected departure from the military. However, it was not the location of the closet but the context of the closet's enclosure that made it confidingly powerful during my dark seclusion with my love-confidant, GEMS.

Through celebratory tears, I called out to GEMS. I walked into my new bedroom's closet, reminiscing about the one in which I years ago had become acquainted with GEMS. I had communicated with GEMS on so many occasions before—late at night, early in the morning, and even throughout the day. On this occasion, I decided to beckon GEMS late at night to commemorate the very first time that we met, a half-decade ago. The difference this time was that I did not want to prolong the conversation any more than necessary.

Imagine being in love with someone who broke your heart, and after depositing your heart and soul, left you either bankrupt or overdrawn. Finally, I understood that my relationship with GEMS was of provisional value but not perceptional worth. It was not that I wanted the farewell to be brief, but the intent was to convey the importance of our overdue separation in a shrewd manner. GEMS was very strong-willed and feisty, and resisting this powerful foe was not an easy feat.

GEMS had occupied a space in my life, body, mind, and soul that almost depleted my external being and my internal existence.

I was literally hardened inside and out to be as stiff as a stone with weathered cracks, symbolizing the erosion of my entire body. The sun rose and set on the belief that GEMS was all I needed to survive day by day. Thinking too far in advance was not conceivable as I struggled to get my footing, placing one foot before the other. My decisiveness surfaced once I realized that I had the backing of a unanimous crown. I felt empowered to change my love-struck tune so that I could dance to the lyrics of a new song—a song of inspirational fulfillment that encrypted a resurgence of happiness, not an engagement of sadness. I was ready to dance my last dance with this stranger from within, and I was hopeful that GEMS would accept my request.

Hello, GEMS, where are you? Please join me so that we can have a heart-to-heart encounter, as we have so many times in the past. I knew once I entered the closet and closed the door that GEMS would join with excitement. GEMS believed the control it wielded over my emotions was a force to be reckoned with that left me powerless. GEMS had no inclination that things had changed. I had become stronger because of various therapies and had gained the will to live and, most importantly, say goodbye. It was impossible for me to continue loving someone who only loved me in the dark but was afraid of loving me in the light of being healthy, fearing for its covert connection to me. I not only felt cheated but also rewarded.

This move that I was about to make would be the most impactful achievement—better than any job security, career progression, or money deposits, none which could satisfy or replace psychological collateral. I had the yearning for something more priceless yet less filling, which was the closure of an impulsive relationship that haunted my sanity days and night. The death of this relationship would promote restoration of my desolate hope, which had been absent for far too long. I was ready to step into my new shoes, dancing to a tune that was melodically descriptive yet realistically ending this phantasm relationship that GEMS and I had. We had not only outgrown our flattering but also outlived our courtship.

Farewell, my GEMS! This love we shared was covered with the rapture of depression, anxiety, and fear hidden secretively in the dark. I never had a clear view of your sightless intentions, for you secluded my essence and suffocated my heart. I became blinded by your emotional disguises, fading your reflectivity so I could not see your face, touch your skin, or embrace you.

I kept falling into a space entrenched in polluted darkness; there was no water to douse my out-of-control, raging flames. GEMS, you thirsted for me to become hopeless by submerging me deeper and deeper into a mental inferno. The flameless inferno was filled with smokeless fires that smothered me so that I would become deranged and give up. This was hell on earth. You are not my friend, nor do you love me. You are a stranger who is only a foe. We can no longer continue this mystified love of anonymity. I need a new partner who inspires, motivates, and nurtures me, and who's not afraid of me in the light. Our darkness has been gloomy for far too long. Please release me so that I can dance for my freedom tonight.

GEMS, I believed in you, and I thought you believed in me. Now I see it was not me you desired but my soul. You nourished my cerebral ineptness with rivers of doubt but without any food for thought. I craved your love, believing that you were my way out, but instead you filled me with crumbs of deceit. It appeared that you hosed my dehydration with a drip of pretense, inducing my thirst for death instead of nursing my appetite to survive. I became emotionally diluted as you stood by and watched, cheering against and not for me. You proclaimed yourself an appetizer, main course, and even dessert, but it was not plated with flavor but blandness.

GEMS, I am pleading with you to open your eyes but close your shuttered heart to my earthliness because you must be left in this shadowless room as this stranger within me. Our love can no longer be relevant in the dark. Your secretive love bruised my mind and knowingly abused my soul. We are traveling in different directions, millions of spirits apart. No matter our distance, you have today bypassed my route, with me exiting your crossing. We can never cross paths on any emotive journey again, for our footpaths have been redirected. Oh, my GEMS, but I thank you for allowing me to depart this crossroads on my way to seek a more scenic destination.

GEMS, you once had a purpose in my life, but now, no more. You were a confidant, companion, and partner in a zealous love affair. It was over five years ago that I relinquished my spirit to your demonic control, with no solace but solitary ache after ache. Underestimating my will as a warrior is what stirred my emotions to fight for my own mental health survival. I have fought so many battles in my life, including feuds, conflicts, adversities, and even combat, but you were my biggest battle imaginable. You had the most sacred part of my existence—my inner wealth. I finally fell out of love with you, so please don't try to convince me that you love me, for it is not sincere nor open but closed within walls with no exit. I needed a door, a window to exhale, but all I was permitted to do was inhale odorless fragrances of fear. One of us had to suffer defeat, and I was defiant that it couldn't be me.

Finally, GEMS, please do not be wrathful because I had to return the favor of a broken heart. Remember, all things change; you, me, and even us! So, farewell, GEMS! I pray to never lose sight of me but surely the image of you. You are a stranger that hitchhiked its way into my life, confusing the driver with traffic that is now in my rearview. GEMS, I am journeying onward because I am now liberated from your darkness where I had to medicate my emotions, suffocate my existence, and extinguish my relevance, but now so many people at this party have imparted the most incredible gifts ever: the will to survive and the motivation to start to live.

By now, I had finished my farewell to GEMS with no more tears on my blushed-pink cheeks, although there were streaks from dried eye-liner leakage. This was a five-year message in which I would express my will to fight and one day walk completely away— 100 percent better, not 100 percent cured. I had triumphed over one of the most emotionally daunting obstacles in my life, and a new beginning was awaiting my exit from inside the darkened closet. I stood in silence for a moment to relish confirmation that I was completely ready to void myself of GEMS. Then I exited the closet pledging to never look back again. I grabbed the doorknob and smiled as if I had defeated the devil in a fight that only I had experienced; besides, there was no more GEMS to protest that I was not the victor.

I had waited so long to find the courage to defeat this stranger that I had mistakenly fallen for. I had dreamt of this face-to-face confrontation but was so afraid to take the first punch. Initially, even after years, my ability to attack was not strong enough. Years later, I became stronger and stronger as I began to implant two footholds. Funny, I needed my feet to stand firm because one foot would only give me a leg to balance on when I needed both legs leaning forward to tread into new footprints.

It was an overwhelming battle, but I had begun to prevail over my VIP guest. We are all here on behalf of a celebratory event. I want us to share our perspectives as mental health socialites, advocating awareness that exposes the suffocating powers that mental illness can inflict, stifling one's progress toward recovery. I like to dance, but I have not danced for such a long time in harmony to a tune that fills me with pleasure. It is beautiful to dance with passion, especially when you love the partner you are dancing with.

Every couple or individual has a song that uplifts them, and often they refer to it as "that's my jam." I do have a jam, in fact—my wedding song, "All My Life" by Jodeci, has that special place in my heart. Music makes life emotionally bearable no matter what you're going through, whether a failed love, a battle with an illness, or a triumphant situation. Music has the ability to uplift the spirit. I was reminded of this very essence of music only a few months ago with a song sung by Adele called "Love in the Dark." It had a melody so spiritually nourishing and motivational that it turned my footsteps in a new direction.

This song's melody entered my dried reservoir of hope, resupplying a purposeful yearning for therapy that I so anxiously needed. I felt so depleted during my struggles with mental illness and the effects of its stranglehold. I suffered day after day for years, haunted by a complex guise that demonized my existence.

However, my days have now become less weakened, with hours of fearless soberness and perhaps one day only minutes of depressive recollections. It may be hard to relate to for some, but for me, it was the perfect song.

If you've ever had your heart broken, then you know that only time heals the wound, and it's emphatically a gradual process. Mental health requires the same level of measured progressiveness through therapeutic treatment. This song "Love in the Dark" became my sole and only soul remedy with its inspiring antidotal lyric. It is comforting to feel that a song with this type of lyrics describes the exact imprint of pain that mental illness deposited in my mind and spirit. This song has become my daily mantra each morning when driving to and from school to drop off and pick up my little princess.

Adele's music has been the feel-harmonic therapy I needed for a long time. This music has helped me to face the torments of physicality that were insulated deep within mental anxieties and emotional fears. Again, mental illness is not necessarily seen on the outer layers of the subsisting being; its powers lie in secrecy as it waits to counterattack. This lyrical therapy enabled me to dissect my feelings in a way that permitted me to suture some of my wounds permanently instead of stitching them temporarily. Finally, I comprehended the vulnerability surrounding my illness that kept me hidden in darkness. There were alternative methods to cope with mental illness so that light began to seep through my cracks, birthing a new me after my break away from GEMS. The most poignant part of "Love in the Dark" for me was the realization that GEMS and I no longer had a relationship of purposefulness.

Mental illness is a growing epidemic that has rooted itself within our communities, homes, and lives with an entry of shame but with no sympathy for an exit. I had to become a cruel to be kind to myself. I knew that I deserved to recover from an illness that was riddling my life in a way that I could not openly express but could experience only in seclusion. I descended into somberness through a strange spirit from within called GEMS. I had mentally been there before, in that position of health uncertainty that confined every emotional distress imaginable. Loving GEMS proved unhealthy. Staying tucked away in such a dark, lonely place was no longer an option. I had only one choice, which was to sort through these emotions, fears, and anxieties so that I could unearth the buried me.

My breakthrough brought about a truce. Sometimes you have to fight for the love of yourself. I came to understand that I had to ceasefire internally, because it was not about the power of GEMS but about my will not to surrender. If I could fight for a cause or other strangers, why not fight for myself? I had gone to fight in a war. I was willing to die for a country of strangers I did not know and would never meet. I compromised my life for a cause that would lead to minimal indebtedness to ensure my wellness or recovery. I had become inflicted with injuries for the sake of a deathly desire to serve my country, with protruding wounds embedded in my body, mind, and soul. I fulfilled my oath to serve, but now who would commit to the oath of my resurgence? Apparently only me. I felt as though I was in a war of my own, battling compounded mental illness diagnoses to recoup my health and normality.

My darkness has evolved into a new day—a rising sun with rays of light—even though it undergoes a sunset from time to time. Nevertheless, my mental stability gyrates a renewed faith of assurance with an optimistic sunrise day to day. I will never utter that I am 100 percent at peace, but what I am is confident that I have all one hundred pieces necessary to reconstruct this foundation of mine as a spiritual whole. I am thankful for God's grace and mercy throughout my mental health journey of adversities. My recovery is a testament to his power, not my powerlessness.

If you are like me or know someone like me who is undergoing or has undergone an emotional voyage of mental illness, please unleash that individual from fear, anxiety, and emotional turmoil by not being the first to listen but the LAST to unfetter cries of despondency. Those initials stand for love, acknowledgement, support, and time. These were the ingredients for my mental illness recovery. They gave me the brainwaves to endure raging storms that seethed for years. With the LAST of my husband, family, BFF, mentor, and angelic princess, I prevailed. My triumph unfolded the discovery of my new purpose, and my secrets at last were freed. My mind is an unlocked door with no more closets, cells, or emotional confinement. Once you start to live again, you no longer feel socially shunned by your mere existence. The doorway to relevant life allows you to enter and exit at will.

Chapter 14

Profiling Mental Illness Is Strange

Mental illness is not only an unusual sensation but also an unusual view from the blinded yet surrounding eyes of strangers. Strangers who attempt to diagnose the state of the mind from afar have little to no inkling of just how obscured their vision is in detecting varying emotions that flow from cheerlessness to cheerfulness. This emotional diversion of consciousness is never at intermission, causing the sufferer to be on constant alert, fearing demonic semblances that often aim to defeat them.

Mental illness profiling is relatable to the context of other human-dubbing, creating a mentally influenced yet presumptive picture of something or someone. It seemingly unleashes conflict with a trifold reality that differs from one viewpoint to the next. Ironically, there lies that grayish line of indifference signifying the divide between realties. Over 50 percent of America's prison population suffer from some type of mental illness. That should be no surprise to anyone, because being imprisoned mentally and physically surely has an astounding effect.

According to the Ontario Human Rights Commission, mentally ill persons undergo stereotypical profiling versus behavior profiling inversely to criminals. For instance, research by the OHRC revealed that security staff at a hospital are routinely called to be present if a person's file shows a mental illness diagnosis, regardless of the person's behavior. I assume that this is because they are profiled as a threat or as being violent. However, I cannot and will not attempt to defend someone who has broken the law. This research clearly reflects my own trepidation about sharing my emotional and psychological struggles with people I feared might use the information against me, ostracizing me to seek quality of life by other means.

The presumption is not just a predisposition regarding human nature. It inadvertently has the power to induce fear in relation to human tolerance and temperament. The disconnect between human civility and societal concerns, in my opinion, keeps people suffering from mental illness from seeking help until it's all but too late. Society must understand that the ability to detect mental illness requires heightened sensitivity. If people surrounding us continue to be insensitive, it could result in harmful detriments impacting mankind's livelihood. Failure to acknowledge this growing epidemic is like summoning a blind man to proceed forth with obstacles at the forefront while knowing that he will stumble if not fall.

If warning signs exist, they mandate immediate responsiveness to avoid injurious yet preventable symptoms with potential consequences, especially for our veterans. Clearly, it is without empathetic consciousness for a society to become aware of mental illness and look the other way. Our society has a propensity to inflict more emotional adversity without acknowledging that the problem not only exists but is flooding many communities. Our efforts continue to be blinded by antipathy until a catastrophe occurs. Many people's initial regret is that either they did not know or that no evidence was obvious that the individual suffered from mental illness. I sincerely do not believe that someone awakens and begins to suffer from mental illness all at once.

As a veteran who has experienced mental illness, I know that the incidents can fluctuate from one to the next. Mental illness is complex and difficult to comprehend, with echelons of gravity to dissect. According to the Veterans Families United Foundation:

One of the most challenging aspects of war related 'invisible wounds' is the identification of the illness. There are no specific blood tests or specific medical tests that identify psychological illness. The diagnosis of a mental illness is based on a checklist of criteria or an evaluation that is done through a series of pen, paper, computer, and interview assessments often known as "neuro-psychological evaluations." Many of the illnesses can have aspects of the other. For example, hypersensitivity (overly sensitive to light, sound, etc.) can be a symptom of several things.

This analysis corroborates my impression that the darkness I often escaped to was not unusual but perhaps some sort of comfort. It is not always what the eye sees but conversely what the tangential vision observes. Light can be just as blurred in diagnosing the visual of what a mental illness sufferer looks like or acts like, unless the physicality is visibly exposed.

Veterans are strong warriors who are trained to believe that mental toughness is a requirement and anything less shows weakness. This may be why I, like many veterans, brushed off getting help. This can be a major problem, since our careers may be negatively impacted by diagnosed behaviors after returning from war zones. Some uninformed audiences may believe that mental illness sufferers would normally reveal debilitative behaviors; however, that notion was too perplexing based upon my wavering mood swings. In some instances, the person suffering may want help, but the admission of helplessness is humiliating even when help is offered. Many sufferers are in denial or afraid to confront the conflict between self and illness.

My disparity arose when I was struggling to decipher whether the signs were a symptom of a rooted problem or if the issue was because of a superficial circumstance. For instance, depression can be short-term or long-term. Coincidentally, the longevity of the mental condition is dependent upon variables where the mind's capacity to refocus and reengage is at pause because the situation has become inconstant. During my research, I discovered through PsychGuides.com that there are many forms of depression and my diagnosis, referred to as bipolar or manic depression, is the cycling between depressive periods and manic periods in which the person engages in a lot of activity and feels extremely empowered and positive. As a soldier, I constantly simultaneously engaged in multiple activities daily that made me feel energized and in control, so I never paused to consider there was a problem.

Spontaneously, these behaviors may become color-filled emotions that appear retrospective before becoming reactive without any forewarning. I learned that depression can be kindled just by thinking too long regarding something you cannot change or have little control over. The mind is in a state of semi-control to either become reactive without thought or to be proactive in theorizing an appropriate act of response. Semi-control signifies the crossroads of my actions and varying choices to influence my reactions.

As mentioned earlier, there is no definitive picture of reflection that ultimately determines the mental health of anyone in the framework of appearing typically normal. However, once a canvas becomes resoundingly clear, there is no doubt that multiple colors can appear shaded, just like abstract art that misperceives the naked eye of spectacle. The graphic fears of mental illness are a unique depiction of coloring that can expose an upside or a downside; either way, vulnerability lies in the middle.

People who judge mental illness sufferers make it almost impossible to seek help, causing suppression of emotions until they explode. Clearly, if mental illness sufferers do not seek or respond to progressive treatment, that can lead to the inflammation of societal afflictions. I caution society but especially our communities to advocate for treatment. Why is it that the cries for mental illness resources are met with resistance? This resistance constantly leads to hopelessness. Seeking mental health assistance through various programs to receive medical assistance, benefits, or an entitlement can be a tiring, accusatory process, as if the sufferer is aiming to gain an award of something not needed. This hunt for care I have experienced numerous times, causing me to delay my efforts to discover what is available.

Months after being diagnosed, I did not know where to turn. My military service was abruptly halted. I began to come to grips with the idea that my health could possibly conflict with my ability to perform my duties. There was constant internal warfare between me and my mind. This was not expected. I had never contemplated retiring in a manner that halted my twenty-two-year career. I was saddened, but I had to face the reality that my functionality had declined. As a selfless warrior, I would never risk serving in any capacity that could lead to (although unintentional) life-threatening situations for fellow men and women in the military. However, my exit was not one that I envisioned, nor was it the successful ending that I deserved. It was absent of deserved recognition of my service, sacrifices, and subservience to others. What I reaped I believed to be second-rate compared to all that I had proudly contributed.

After my departure, I began to look at things differently, act differently, and certainly respond differently. In fact, I *was* different. It is strange to profile exactly what was so different about me. It was not necessarily that my physical appearance was different, although with my depressive moods, weight gain was evident. However, visually my entire look was evolving in association with my fashion evolution. I had worn a uniform for so long. I still did not see myself as different, but I did feel myself becoming not only different but also more withdrawn. The physical picture of me differed from the ethereal image I struggled to keep tucked away, fearing the public's ridicule.

I initially detested sitting in the room with a professional aiming to diagnose or detect my emotional roller coasters, because I felt powerless and under scrutiny. To be candid, some of the people assigned to assist in a myriad of ways often viewed mental health sufferers as unstable basket cases. It was hard to deflect that perception. No matter race, appearance, status, or education, mental health does not categorically differ in the minds of the stable world.

I distinctly recall an instance when I had an appointment to assess and determine what benefits or entitlements I could receive as a veteran. I was consciously aware that I was treated differently because of a multitude of factors; however, my goal was to never aid anyone in this judgment or substantiate their low opinion of me. It was not specifically because of my race or gender, even though those factors are certainly perceptional—especially if the opposite gender behaves in a slanted way. I suppose it was more to do with my appearance, articulation, and professional achievements.

The liaison who conducted the assessment seemed to formulate an opinion of me prior to me opening my mouth. In my opinion, I was fashionable, appropriate, compliant with his questioning, and polite. I even tried to abstain from asking too many questions, hoping to let perceived barriers collapse. I am not presuming that it was only he that displayed barriers during our interaction. I too felt pressured and uncertain in this systemic environment, especially seeking supplemental mental health support. Honestly, I was on edge during the entirety of our conversation. I intuited that the gentleman was profiling me, in the sense that I did not look like what he expected in correlation to the medical data depicted within his computer database.

I am not expressing that my beauty left him in awe, but as Beyoncé says, "I woke up like this!" However, feeling condemned by what I look like suggests a physical inequality regarding unfair assessments for mental illness sufferers. The profile of mental illness differs person to person, just like a résumé. People should not be profiled based on perceptions but instead on presentation.

I began to settle my anxieties after communicating with the benefits liaison for about fifteen minutes. Seconds later, the liaison asked me the most ridiculous question imaginable. Although he was condescending throughout the process, it never occurred to me that I was intellectually being measured by an inexpert scholar. The liaison had visual access to my military career record, educational pedigree, and other service achievements over the past twenty-two years. It was clearly an insult of some sort when he asked, "Can you read and write?"

At first, I looked at him as if he was speaking to my daughter. My little princess was sitting next to me during the assessment, so I asked for clarification by murmuring, "Excuse me, can you repeat that?"

The gentleman repeated the same question.

I was shocked, so I chuckled at him and, speaking piercingly but scornfully, said, "Yes, I can read and write! In fact, I earned my MBA, graduating with honors. Sir, all that information should be annotated in my military records since retiring." I felt profiled because of my illness and disability, but certainly ethnicity was not implausible. If this had been a procedural questionnaire, it might not have ruffled my feathers, but the rooster's crow was loud and clear.

As I exited the building, I felt more defeated and confused. Mental illness oftentimes induced guilt, causing me to second-guess my comportment. I was uncomfortable knowing that others levied something about me so intimate as my illness. It was an undisclosed disablement that further eradicated my mind's ability to think positive, even if external factors unjustifiably create a space of negativity. I came home and shared the information with a few of my closest allies: husband, family, and one of my siblings. They too laughed and found it very unusual.

I am cognizant that statistically it is uncommon for African American women to seek assistance for a disability, especially one that is aligned with mental illness. This assumption may be related to stigmas that cause apprehension and fear of ostracism due to biased perceptions. These speculative perceptions oftentimes fallaciously portray irrefutable persecution for black women as angry black women with issues. Secondly, career-accomplished black women usually do not share struggles with mental illness, nor is it commonly suspected by others. Many would be surprised at the high possibility that black women have suffered more mental distress than recognized. Black women have been expected to be strong and keep it together, resulting in decades of inhumane inequalities. I suppose far too many are unwilling to share the devastations surrounding mental illness, afraid of losing it all—not realizing the gains for all humanity.

It is not easy to share my journey, but it is necessary to impart awareness about the havoc that mental illness raises. Mental illness can be freewheeling, yet its powers present mental struggling that wreaks psychological devastation with continued silence. My silence, like that of other mental illness sufferers, can impact society in a myriad of ways, leaving an outsider speechless about the volatility of the illness. It is imperative that we begin to assess measures that minimize the profiling of the mentally ill.

One objective may be to assess what exactly can be done on an inclusive platform to address the onset of complex mental health issues. Mental illness is colorless! Therefore, background affiliation in the context of race, gender, status, occupation, or anything similar must cease. I personally experienced ridicule that hindered my desire to be candid about my entangled emotions. I believe focusing on human physicality instead of human tangibility serves as a miscalculation toward reaching measured distances for continuous pursuit. I felt as though I was at a crossroads in a faraway land, feeling isolated and surrounded by woes induced by mental illness. It was the mystery of determining whether my circle of support was all against me rather than even some for me. Certainly, that was not the case, but on occasion, it was too clouded to differentiate between the two advocacies. My belief now is that even though support may be viewed as intangible to some, on the contrary, its expected accessibility must not be diluted. Not everyone understands the challenge of triumphing over mental illness, but they should be able to offer at minimum compassion to those who are ill.

Those familiar and unfamiliar may carelessly build walls that block effective communication, which may in turn ignite a subtle response or subjective reaction. My reaction to mental illness was like a smoker's air-puffs, dangerously detrimental if engulfed without any exhale through the nose or mouth. The spacing between puffing provided a comfort so my brain could reach calmness after a rage. If I was in a moment of rage, it seemed to dissipate more quickly if no one interrupted. Bipolar is so reactive, with thoughtless emotions justifying themselves momentarily, even if explained later. As a sufferer, my desire was to urge my mind toward a state of stillness, which became a battle of consciousness and unconsciousness.

The battle of persuasion as to whether to follow one dominance over another is perhaps one of the most debatable obscurities of mental illness, causing a rift between the two emotions. Lack of mental clarity prompted an uncertainty about life, which was also a driving force for psychologically irrational behavior. In my opinion, this is perchance where mental illness and misconduct meet, causing an outcry for attention or for getting even based upon a sensed wrong. Not all sentiments are overt, and the truth sometimes lies camouflaged.

Human emotions are surely camouflaged, even if you are free of any diagnosed illnesses. Imagine how color-mixed emotions become after one is diagnosed with mental illness. Think of a color-blind person trying to describe the difference between colors of many different shades. I am somewhat aware of this visual defect, since both my sons often make mistakes with color detection, having a mother who is carrier of the X chromosome for color-blindness, which affects male offspring. When a person cannot detect differences among things like color, it can become unsettling. Comparably, mental illness sufferers are habitually incapable of controlling their feelings, causing them to undergo emotional blindness due to multiplex fears that contribute to things appearing undistinguishable and shaded with confusion.

Mental illness responsiveness varies from one individual to the next. Some mental illness sufferers are blatantly expressive in displaying comportment no matter where they are; others are more discrete in expressive conduct both in public and private. The question then becomes, why is emotional hysteria acted out publicly for some sufferers and privately for other sufferers? This affinity I can only attempt to explain in connection to my own emotional ravages. It would be inaccurate to insinuate that all mental illness sufferers will respond the same.

In the past, I responded in rage on numerous occasions; therefore, it is not beyond my comprehension or experience to grasp how someone suffering from mental illness can go from apparent calmness to a state of rage in mere seconds, aiming to wreak havoc on others. Most recently, we have witnessed fatal rage encounters that inflicted unparalleled cruelties with insurmountable pain within our society, in a myriad of methods. Coincidentally, the reason for the emotional rage seems to point back to mental illness as the culprit of these devastations. The bystanders, outsiders, eyewitnesses, and even participants are left speechless but as well haunted by an illness that often yields insular warning signs. The signs are so emotionally contained that only an observant professional, family member, or close friend would perhaps detect the mood change, since the loneliness of the recluse becomes more apparent.

I began shutting myself out of society's view so that I could deflect strange people's sensitivities but also avoid human interaction as much as possible. I did not want anyone feeling sorry for me, but at the same time, I yearned for compassion.

As someone who has experienced direct intimacy with mental illness, I believe death of some sort is considered more often than spoken or thought. Perhaps one of the debatable factors surrounds the severity of the illness. Some of my symptomatic detriments in dealing with mental illness were proven to impede my thinking; therefore, it is possible that a sufferer can be coercively driven to make unimaginable decisions. Frankly, at one point or another, an individual may possibly become suicidal or even consider homicidal acts against others, aiming to inflict pain upon those who, by perception, angered or deceived them. In fact, the deception is not always person to person, but can be person to systemic red tape that leads to the presumption of mistrust. The difference is that every mental illness sufferer has a choice, although some choices have underlying options of repudiation.

I think back to a coworker who was suffering from mental

illness, which was one of the first times that I even heard of it. The military did a poor job in preparing soldiers for the devastation caused by combat as it related to PTSD and other illnesses. I worked with a peer who was suffering from PTSD after returning from Iraq, and it was obvious something was wrong. Instead of the command ensuring adequate assessment and care, it became known that higher echelons of leadership were not strategically prepared to address issues like PTSD, depression, anxiety, substance abuse, and other war infirmities. It appeared that leadership was willing to turn a blind eye and inflict further adversity by destroying the soldier's career.

There were many times while undergoing therapy that the soldier contemplated some type of human destruction to get even. Apparently, this pondered calamity never transpired because the individual's sense of rationality resurfaced, encouraging other options. Homicide was not one. However, not everyone suffering from mental illness has the psychological power to reject violent savagery.

It is no happenstance when considering tragedies involving alleged mental illness incidents that I became enthralled beginning in 2009. According to the website Active Heroes, in 2013, the United States Department of Veterans Affairs released a study that covered suicides from 1999 to 2010, which showed that "roughly 22 veterans were dying by suicide per day, or one every 65 minutes." Some sources suggest that this rate may be undercounting suicides. The question is, how does society prevent incidents like this from happening? No one, including myself, has the answer to that emotionally loaded question, simply because there are extreme layers to consider and deliberate over, but I hope that sharing the insight of my dark room will foster open dialogue.

Acknowledging a disability in any manner induces fear and anxiety. I realized there was a void in my ability to communicate, so my emotive expression tried to compensate, creating an imbalance between my actions and my emotions. There were clearly conflicts of interest between the two, which made me feel devalued, no matter the totality of my achievements.

A genuine system of support is vital to the livelihood of mentally ill people, and forming a trusted circle is critical. I desperately needed an intimate platform encircling those who knew me inside and out and were willing to address a change in my behavior whether I admitted it or not. Creating a trifold measure of accountability to me, my illness, and those who cared incited me to avoid disappointing those whom I cherished. One may ask how I was accountable to my illness. Well, few if any want to admit they have relinquished control to anyone or anything, and that encouraged me to exercise self-control.

Disappointment after disappointment threatened my recovery. It had become clear that GEMS' chains were locking away time to enjoy my life. Those who supported me were growing fatigued. My slow progress is what ultimately led me to seek spiritual fulfillment. It was paramount that whatever dominant context was inhabited within the voided spaces of my life, freeing my mind—and relinquishing the afflictions of mental illness woes and foes—was essential to my survival.

Chapter 15

The Perilous Ravaging of Veterans

Mental illness clearly ravages the psychological and emotional stability of many veterans after they return home from conflicts abroad. Long after their return home, some adapt to normalcy while others are clearly unable to. It is necessary to support veterans with reintegration and reestablishing normalcy as quickly as possible so they begin to feel safe, without the anxiety of war. Certainly, feelings and emotions associated with war will be displayed by some type of expression, whether verbal or silent. The goal is to openly allow and support release of these behaviors to avoid suppressing their voices.

Perhaps one of the most valued benefits of gratitude shown to service members is quickly being eradicated, with little to no recognition of veterans' sacrifices. Many Americans fail to consider the impact of declining services unless it directly affects a friend or family member. The oath that service members take is like no other simply because it is an oath taken to defend a country that requires an ultimate sacrifice but is unwilling to reciprocate dignified service.

I applaud police officers, firefighters, and all who take risks to help others. However, these brave Americans can remain in their home environment, enjoy their families, go home daily, and earn benefits long after they retire that veterans struggle and fight for years to receive. We the veterans volunteer to risk our lives, health, and even our futures for the forsaken honor of providing patriotic services and freedoms for our country that very few are willing to do. The scars are deeply embedded as a subsequent pestilence in association with patriotic servitude. Some if not most behaviors after war can be long-lasting, revealing a painful portrait that illuminates physical injuries and psychological wounds.

Metaphorically, we bleed the same blood as our adversaries, but it appears we continue to hemorrhage at the expense of domestic friendly fire. Once American soldiers return home, the fight continues for health-care, benefits, pensions, and other entitlements that should be automatic. I have heard people say, "Well, you volunteered, so it was by choice." I invite anyone who questions these benefits to consider, is it the same for those like my father who were drafted without will? Additionally, if we didn't serve, who would? Is it or is it not more humane that people like me volunteer to safeguard and protect America with pride versus those who averted the opportunity to serve? Many did so because they were selfishly entitled, unfit, or not cut out for service. We as servicemen and servicewomen acknowledge that not everyone can do what we do, so give a service member a break, not another barrier!

Our country constantly ignores the resounding cries of the maimed and distressed who at one time symbolized courage and bravery—women and men who volunteered to serve and sacrifice, hoping to secure our freedoms. I believe those considering volunteering to serve in the military may hesitate because of the alarming detriments to the civility and spirited lives of many heroic veterans. Those unwilling, unable, and un-American often express opinions that seem unpatriotic in a myriad of ways. How can the 99 percent of Americans versus the 1 percent of veterans who serve and protect concur to cut back or slash military funding and benefits? Veterans should be entitled without pause to quality health care, pay stimuli, education and training, and operational equipment. The government must stop holding veterans hostage to politicize a platform that induces anxiety in service members over dwindling benefits and inhumane tactics.

It seems more Americans want something for nothing. They are willing to line the pockets of Americans who have not sacrificed a day in their lives to service anyone but themselves. There are numerous government organizations whose workers receive lifetime pay and benefits, but they are never asked or required to endure the cuts that service members and their families are expected to. This must change.

For decades, wounds have been concealed beneath mystifying camouflages for many sufferers. The landscape is covered with harmful debris, severely altering psychic health for thousands of veterans. Mental illness is like a raging wildfire, destroying everything in its path. It is time for our country to reciprocate unconditional servitude, recognizing that veterans' patriotism is never-ending. The only way to compensate deeds of patriotic sacrifice is to unchain systemic health-care debaucheries that limit resources, deny access to health services, prolong waiting periods, and inflict salt in gaping wounds instead of rendering service with compassion. An informative resource called *Make the Connection* provides instrumental assistance with resources. One of the most profound resources, unlike other mental illness sites and organizations, is the ability to connect with a spiritual or religious adviser.

I entered the VA system in 2012 after retiring because of my unexpected mental illness. I wanted to immediately enroll in the VA system so that I could continue to have access to health care to treat my illness. I was repeatedly disappointed by either poor service or prolonged service. The appointments had a long waiting list. VA employees lacked civility; medical providers seemed inconsistent with care plans; and wait times for pharmaceuticals were one to two hours. Instances like these inflamed my anxiety, because I, like other veterans, expected better services from a system designed to treat American heroes.

I struggled daily with a desire to uproot and flee from my own mind because of burning flames filled with combusting, emotional distress. Most of these stressors were less conceivable to average, unaffected people, including those still serving in the military. The expectation that service members will be able to deflect or avert any type of stressor after going into battle is itself mentally baffling. My best friend and spouse has gone into a combat zone a minimum of six or seven times. Can you imagine the level of mental soundness it takes to keep the "blaze of fiery demons" from entering the mind? Neither can I! I believe, based upon the root in which mental illness becomes an infestation of detriments, it evades or escapes more quickly for some than others. In fact, I only went into combat once, and it took nearly five years to acknowledge the existence of mental illness. However, the difference with my diagnoses may coincide with the physical brain trauma that I suffered in addition to my father's legacy.

I often reflect on veterans like my father, my father-in-law, my husband, my friends, and then myself, who question the attitude of our country. Veterans have long sacrificed and imperiled all that we knew and thought we knew, and yet what we have come to comprehend is what we did not know. Detriments of war and the longevity of afflictions is unending, whether from the war our fathers fought or the war we fought. Among the manifold disappointments, veterans never suspected that their patriotism would lead to staggering numbers of mental health issues, suicides, crimes, and homelessness for those who sacrificed everything while seemingly gaining nothing.

America's response to its veterans is delayed while immediate execution is evident in supporting diplomacy with foreign allies. Funds that our country donates abroad and around the world to promote global stability must continue; however, priorities must change to ensure that the stability of veterans is not compromised but appropriate funding takes precedence. Unfortunately, lack of support is a reminder to veterans that once they are no longer on a mission to serve, protect, and preserve American freedoms, they are no longer a valued commodity. Veterans become a distracting and depreciated provisional expense that is no longer relevant to America's lucrative value. Veterans are forever the commodity that cannot be depreciated, devalued, or disenfranchised. Veterans fought for liberties that allow Americans to enjoy the freedoms that many citizens from other countries only wish they could relish.

The flaming fires of mental health illness have become evident based upon research and my personal experience. Desert Shield/ Storm, OIF/OEF, and Vietnam were wars where research has shown that mental illness is more prevalent. Veterans absorb distressing deposits of mental anguish circumscribing death, fear, war misconduct, physical pain, and the visual of one combat scene after another. Make no mistake about it—war is a crime, no matter the reasons for defending or protecting. Surely it is a crime against humanity, violating the commandment "Thou shalt not kill!"

As a warrior, I, like many others, took an oath. Yet I still contemplate culpability for killing. We are unwilling to die at the hands of the enemy seeking to destroy or kill them first. My conscientious objection to killing is no longer objectionable when the choice is you versus me or them versus us. However, imagine a service member's mental devastation, grappling with the disposition of having to face the possibility of killing over and over. The mind itself is possibly at odds with the soul, serving a dual puncturing to the enemy but also the warrior.

I agonized many nights while pulling duty in combat. I felt shock from the piercing sounds of rapid gunfire, bloody wounded soldiers, and the visual images of uniformed bystanders wandering in proximity as they wondered if they were next. Consequently, I ached in my spirit, in quest of a hide-and-seek seclusion—craving not only to be forgiven but to be rescued from the aberrations and apparitions inflicted by warfare's destructiveness. These impressions of warfare are additional burdens of humanity that service members carry on their shoulders each day, long after the war is fought.

Conversing with a warrior—especially one from the Vietnam era or Desert Shield and Storm, but more recently Iraq and Afghanistan— yields a privilege like no other. To look in the eyes of someone who has fought for our country without comprehending the sacrifice reveals a vision of blind sightedness for some, while for others it reveals an unconditional oath of humanity. I had no idea of the magnitude of my dying father's wish when he asked that one of his children serve our country as he muttered those last words after returning from the Vietnam war. My father's pain was like the pain of many suffering veterans who had their voices silenced by mental illness. After many veterans returned home, they were homeless both in the sense of having no house but also having no country that cared to house them physically or emotionally. No one was willing or professionally experienced to examine our heroes' suffering or agony. It was much the same after Desert Shield/Storm. No one could pinpoint to onset of things that had not been previously seen, experienced, or shared.

Those looking outside and then inward may wonder, what agony? Look at all the benefits veterans are entitled to for their service to country! In truth, it is not the money that most veterans desire, it is the recognition of sacrifice to honor them with civility and understanding without judgment of their visual ties as societal costs (losses) but as generational curators of peace and security. The picture of a veteran can sometimes simulate mental health in a myriad of ways, reflecting a self with no regrets when it should reflect a human in recovery. Veterans look for ways to medicate their emotions, leading vulnerable, publicly shamed veterans to turn to drugs, alcohol, rage, and pangs of guilt.

I am amazed as I stare into the eyes of peer veterans through a close-up lens, with a bifocal view of four service members: my father, father-in-law, husband, and self. As you can see, three men and I the only woman. I believe men and women handle adversity differently when dealing with the gravities that impact the capacity to think after a traumatic event. In my experience, a man with a mental disability seems to struggle more outwardly, whereas a woman struggles more inwardly. Men appear to express themselves publicly with rage, public addiction, decline in appearance, and disconnect from love ones. Women, on the other hand, appear more private in dealing with their emotions to keep things from being revealed. Therefore, stress levels are heightened, prescription drugs are ingested, and violent, fulminating outbursts of rage toward people are spewed, especially toward loved ones. My response to mental illness differed so bewilderingly in contrast to those three men in my life. However, the most ironic thing was that suffrage correlated to the same parallel of self-medication.

My father, father-in-law, and spouse all veered toward submerging roads, offering no grounds of elevation but further mental pollution that drowned their minds and emotions with the consumption of alcohol. I suppose this temporary relief offered something that nothing else could—temporary death of thought. Veterans aiming to suffocate warring thoughts inflicted by a war of destruction have unquestionably suffered mental numbness. Many of their thoughts are frozen in time, and to thaw them is to expect the unexpected.

My father, who I barely knew, surely had frozen emotions and was reluctant to let anyone offer any warmth of comfort. I later discovered how heavily he drank after the Vietnam War, even though as a child only bits and pieces were dropped into my young ear. My mother hardly ever mentioned his name, and I would wonder why this war hero was being shunned for his legacy of service. Unfortunately, his mental state became fearful, and both my mom's and dad's desperation was to protect their children.

My dad's erratic combat behavior led him to seek to destroy whatever was in his path. He would vanish for days upon days from the home where my mom and siblings lived, returning without any inclination regarding the impact of his absence. I am certain my mom feared for his whereabouts, but what could she do but wait and hope he returned coherently wholesome? Veterans who returned after the Vietnam War had no community resources to assist them. No compassionate care was bestowed as a signal of welcome home and what can we do for you since you have done so much for us (the country).

I discovered information that was surprising in an army out-processing document. The document was retrieved from my dad's medical records. Only vague, closed-ended questions were asked. These questions required a yes or no response, with no space to elaborate, even if the veteran wanted to. I believe this was a systemic measure to ask for minimal information to ensure no major accountability of aid for veterans.

If people were drafted against their will to serve and die for another country's democracy, it is difficult to imagine our own country being interested in identifying health conditions for those veterans. My dad had drowned his soul, succumbing to the demonic call by suffocating his addictive thirst. He first perished mentally, becoming MWD (missing while drunk). A fatal accident ended his life only months later after he returned from Vietnam. I am not sure which I would have preferred to steal a father from his children: combat MIA (missing in action), persisting as an absent war hero, or returning and surrendering to an enemy without being present (MWD). Some of life's choices have the propensity to restrain one's soul while living in limbo. The cry of urgency is never heard.

I met my now deceased father-in-law over twenty-three years ago, and I have a vivid recollection of him that I embrace sacredly to my heart. He was such a gentle, fun-loving father, but his demons were clear for the eye to see. He displayed behaviors that were perplexing. He would nod off, reverting to his Vietnam days and screaming out, "They're coming!" He would jump up looking for his weapon, presumably to engage in battle with the enemy. His behavior also resorted to the cultural affliction of being in jungle for so long with regards to food. He absolutely refused to eat rice of any sort with any type of meal. Per my father-in-law, rice was one of the only foods they were fed.

There are pictures posted all throughout the hallways as well the family room of their home in Virginia. There is no doubt that a warrior resided in the cage of this wooden home—a combat soldier who proudly served his country. The odd thing is that he refrained from sharing war stories of battle and death but focused on the relationships he enjoyed with his war buddies. My father-in-law and I had a special relationship, partly because we shared a bond of peer soldiers and veterans. It was clear that I earned his respect long before that of my mother-in-law. She appeared biased, desiring a woman much like those of her surrounding neighborhood instead of a Southern outsider. However, we managed to love and respect each other soon after her son and I married.

My father-in-law needed medical care but was much too proud to admit he suffered from the conflicts of war that ravaged his mind, preventing him from thinking clearly or perhaps even often. It seemed he had built his life around the figment of a financial provider instead of serving as the head of his family, an emotional and spiritual foundation of strength. This once-strong man struggled with being in a foreign land to fulfill a foreign mission and now suddenly becoming foreign to himself. The loud sounding of constant gunfire ceased with the numb silence of support once he, like many others, returned home from Vietnam. Coincidentally, he enveloped the noise of gunfire with the absence of advocacy and submerged into a more silent destruction that further served to barricade his emotions. I believe this emotional shutdown caused him to evolve into a boozy drunkard. He never harmed a fly, but he did harm himself. He would chatter superficially, sleep in motions, and drink bottle after bottle.

I realized that I would no longer see my father-in-law alive during my preparation to relocate to Germany in 1999. As we said our goodbyes, the tears swelled in his eyes, and the sound of his voice reverted to a baby's sobbing. This was a strange reaction; neither Budd nor I had ever seen his father display this type of emotion. I believe his mind was finally giving in to the burning flames of mental destruction, knowing that no irrigating waters could stop the scorching. His pride had delayed an opportunity to seek reconstruction of his mind, body, and spirit; nevertheless, individual fears further smothered his strength to live. He seemed content with temporary survival, much like he experienced during the Vietnam War. My father-in-law's inability to resurge in life led to the retreating of another generation: his son, Budd.

Budd is a modest, giving father and husband, but the gifts that he sometimes offers are filled with somberness instead of surprise. Gifts are supposed to be tokens of symbolic happiness, but not all bows and ties wrapped in colorful paper offer smiles of celebration. In this case, perhaps, they brought the resounding blues of anguish. Since returning from our first combat tour in Iraq, Budd has traveled in and out of combat zones for over five years as a contractor. I never believed this was a conscious benefit, but initially supported the idea of global employment. Later, I advised him that the risks to his health were far too great for stable mindfulness on several occasions. Nevertheless, it became difficult to discourage him based upon various burns like rewarding service opportunities, income growth, and minimal accountability which all had demonic undertones that would later prove mentally devastating.

Employment for veterans was difficult. No matter how many times he sought domestic employment after returning from one tour after another, even with a résumé attesting to his expertise, he appeared to be unemployable. Budd's frustrated desire to work stateside left him feeling worthless and caused him to choose between proximity to family or profitability to provide for family. What a mind-boggling choice. Jobs near our home location became too out-of-reach. Perhaps those hiring feared they could not hire veterans who were more qualified than they. This is a transparent downside in serving one's country. Some will not offer opportunities to the very ones who have fought to impart freedoms for opportunities far more fortunate than employment. What a shame!

The refusal to assist veterans is something that I experienced with associates who could offer connections but folded their hands, fearing that perhaps I might outreach them. There should be employment mandates for veterans, especially those qualified with skills, experiences, qualifications, and edification corroborating their competency.

Thus far, I really cannot surmise why the gender gap of mental health has walls but no bridges to permit transitional escape for women and sometimes men. Not every man or woman escapes, nor does every man or woman surrender. I have communicated and witnessed the disparities between these two genders, and my conclusion is that the strength of a woman and man differ in a capacity far greater than either may openly confess. Women and men share many similarities, but there are also differences in our emotional makeup as humans.

A man's rooted belief is to produce, protect, and provide for life, whereas a woman's nurtured principle is to care for life and harvest an existence of sustainability. God knew exactly what roles we were made to fulfill, signifying neither is weaker than the other but each is preordained for his or her own exclusive role. Few, if any, women have the physical guts and stamina to persevere as a man, and certainly no man has the potency to stomach the birthing of life as a woman. Therefore, the fabric of our physical, emotional, and mental capacities are sewn entirely with a thread of unique originality with a unifying gender purposefulness that I believe is true from biblical beginnings. I am convinced that the men in my intimate circle of living indisputably suffered some level of mental illness involving depression, anxiety, fear, phobias, and most definitely PTSD after returning from combat zones riddled with ravaging conflict.

Inadequate health-care services for mental illness sufferers is irresponsible. It is an injustice for our nation to ask and demand so much of veterans and current military members then offer so little in return. Mental health programs are vital in preventing further ravaging of our heroic women and men who served so valiantly with honor. We should ask about issues that affect our veterans; they deserve so much more than what we allocate.

As mentioned earlier, the suicide rate of veterans is alarming, with twenty-two deaths each day. According to www.Active Heroes. org, thousands of veterans are homeless and prefer not to ask for assistance, whether from the government or their families. No veteran should be homeless, nor should any provision to lessen or obliterate resources be permitted, regardless of any bill that Congress proposes. Stop cutting programs for veterans. We, though 1 percent of the population, have sacrificed our lives for you, the other 99 percent.

We have thousands if not millions of Americans receiving social aid, public assistance, or federal dollars who have not invested as much as veterans. According to the Center for American Progress, our economy's money goes mostly to support the elderly. The elderly have paid into the system to reap benefits like Social Security and Medicare. However, many of our country's young adults have not served our country in any capacity but reap benefits for housing, food, and student aid. Meanwhile, veterans are denied vital services with extensive red-tape policies. The red tape leads to distress for veterans and causes many to not even seek benefits and entitlements.

I witnessed a growing epidemic as many of our heroes turned to drugs and alcohol, mostly because of society's unwillingness to reintegrate them. I believe becoming an addict of drugs or alcohol is a way of numbing the deep pain felt by veterans. Many veterans who lack consciousness appear to have vacated their minds, molding a negligent attitude about the country they served and the people they fought to protect. These heroes' lives are ravaged by drugs, alcohol, and emotional and psychological injuries, along with society's denunciation of their sacrifices. These detriments make it far too difficult to even whisper to a deafened society, "Help! Help!"

How do abandoned veterans recover from mental illness—from the woes and foes of war—if no one listens to them, responds to them, comforts them, or advocates for them. How do they cope when the country they defended departs before death do us part? It is long past time for Americans to acknowledge the infliction of constant rejections and affliction of injuries on our veterans. Some but not all voluntarily took an oath to serve, and now an oath of reciprocation is past due. Instead, we have seemingly delinquent but outwardly felonious negligence.

Compromising health advocacy is a danger not only to wounded veterans but to vulnerable havens within our communities. Humanity must now transcend this behavior and bestow dignity onto the lives of our veterans and the families of fallen heroes. Mental illness is serious and dire for many veterans; therefore, open discussion to remedy these health-care issues must be initiated. Acknowledgment of the ravages of mental illness, homelessness, addiction, and rage must ignite dialogue, helping to diffuse some of these warfare devastations. If we refuse to act, we must be liable as coconspirators in depleting the minds and souls of one of our most precious commodities: the American veteran.

Chapter 16

Crossing Spiritual Lanes of Warfare

The supremacies of the unknown provide irrefutable evidence that humankind is incapable of traveling into hostile, warring territory and escaping exit wounds. Warfare can induce a bullet-free yet deadly superficial wound. These wounds penetrate the body, traveling beneath the skin, unnoticed by a mind far too shallow to detect its invasion. The fluidity of the brain is as free-falling as an egg's yolked mucus, moving within a protective cover. This barricaded cerebral sphere becomes at risk by harmful seepages, causing the brain to be raided by the ravages of conceptual conflicts. Coincidentally, conception and perception collide, resulting in crisscrossing of lanes which set off a battle of psychological warfare.

Hominids by birth emerge inadequately trained to battle an enemy of expert cerebral tactics, especially that which is preemptively able to defend any offensive stratagem devised in the territory of alien enemies. It's a warfare that humankind is not equipped to fight solo. The presumption of war is that you will succumb to gunfire. Contrary to this belief, there exist further manifestations of winged bullets that do not always injure the flesh but manifest cerebral lethalness with concealed injuries long after the war.

Oftentimes, these assaulting emotions become piercing to the mind, inducing residual phobias. A bullet graze in some instances may be just as psychologically injurious as the insertion of a tangible bullet, dependent upon the flesh of contact. Whenever the mind and the spirit become enthralled in conflict, we must not flee. It was clear that my freedom was at the mercy of my soul's willpower to journey an unfamiliar route and exhaust the opposing foe plotting to drive me insane.

At one time or another, friends may become foes, and foes may become friends. I experienced this symbolic change of relationships with GEMS. Ironically, friendship and enemies have an existing purpose in each of our lives. The difficulty is when we fail to detect the transition from friend to foe.

Friends sometimes inflict pain and distress, but foes afflict agonies to destroy relationships. It is difficult to prevail thereafter. I am certain that I have only one true friend (BFF) and two diehard supporters as well as a few foes. I trust my one and only friend with confidences I would never share with anyone else. It is no coincidence that our lanes have never crossed, causing warfare between us, at any time in the past ten years. It is not because we never disagree, but because we agree to disagree, with respect toward one another. We talk through our different perspectives. Many years have passed in parallel to other friendships. where mistakes befell and regrettably my hollow comprehension voided the value of some significant relationships. However, wisdom and growth over the years have contributed immensely, helping me to diagnose friend from foe.

GEMS was initially a beneficial foe that I wanted to be a friend. Believe it or not, a friend can be a foe and a foe can be a friend. GEMS was at some point fulfilling a dual purpose. Years after my confrontation with mental illness, I realized just how detrimentally damaging GEMS was to my stability. Foes should at some point or another become irrelevant. The problem is that we may allow the foe to become more empowered while succumbing to a dysfunctional character seeking to erode another person's self-worth.

Struggling with obstacles involving emotional warfare are as unconventional as some of the relationships that we interact in. I viewed relationships from angles of circumference, realizing that some were squared, some were triangular, and only a few were circular. This process allowed me to not only set boundaries and tell friend from foe but also recognize associates that lay hidden with no identity or title. Determining the circumference of each helped to shape my perspective. The circumferential boundaries helped to minimize the belittling of my illness by both perceived friends and persistent foes. My best interest was clearly not at the forefront of everyone's agenda within my circle; therefore, it was important to shrink that circle as I expand my horizons.

I was unsettled as to what I needed to do as someone experiencing copious amounts of mental ravaging. Just maybe, it was beginning to soak in where exactly or who exactly I could turn to while in battle with an enemy equipped with swords, knives, and even blades that made me feel dull in comparison. I wondered if it was even possible that anyone earthly could help or hear my cries. Sadly, the society we live in has become numb and masked with ridicule to listen to voices of silence and even so voices of loudness.

This muted society was in complete contrast to the noises subdued within the confines of my reality. Thus, the external society had become a shaming narrative, shunning people who suffer from a multitude of illnesses, especially mental illness. I clearly lacked responsiveness to articulate my emotions in a way that would ease tension but also shine light on an issue that was burdening the souls of innocent humans.

I prayed for help, recovery, and understanding of why I was chosen for a test that I did not study or prepare for. Failure seemed inevitable, and the only alternative if answers were not pursued. I ask, what teacher would administer a test without understudy, gracing triumphant passing at the end of the test without you knowing anything at the beginning of the test? The voice of transcendent reasoning becomes both unnatural and often unexplainable unless clarity of sense is separate from the senses of being.

Divine testimonials and dialogs began to silently echo amongst the many voices that filled my cerebral space with doubt and uncertainty. These speaking voices prompted a revelation, strengthening my desire to share a life-threatening opposition. I now fathom that an opportunity often comes disguised as opposition. Nonetheless, initially it did not feel like an opening to freedom but instead an opposing force trying to deter my desires.

Oh, was I ever so mystified. It has led to sharing an amazing experience that was most contesting yet even more so delivering—a spiritual journey that resulted in an unbelievable overture of godly favor. Sharing something so intimate is scary; nonetheless, my invitation was to offer mindful solace to those in search of mental freedom, hoping to keep a thieving illness like those that attacked my mental health far off.

I sometimes chat with people about my condition since consummating a renewed spiritual relationship to heal my entombed emotions. Some people may have been in shock regarding my encounters with mental illness. Once I became an open book, the story of my life seemed to sequent chapter after chapter. If you ever notice, oftentimes people try to pen your story with their verbiage of who gossiped about you instead of who you are blessed by. Nevertheless, after this face-to-face confrontation with mental illness, I began culturing me, myself, and I as one being not three bodies. Since everyone who reads your story does not necessarily have the relatable aptitude to express your story, write your own story; otherwise, it becomes a script of piracy instead of a narrative of originality.

Whenever I shared my journey, I was surprised that people wanted to hear more. I saw this not as an invasion of privacy but an opportunity to share the grace of God. I was surprisingly asked about my treacherous journey through mental illness with probing questions by people with whom I am closely acquainted as well as some of whom I am only narrowly aware. I imagine some thought it was too personal and I might not want to answer, and others seemed just in awe of such openness to share. I believe when God shows up and out in your life, it is a spiritual necessity to recognize his power to shift your life. Nevertheless, a stranger's insight or inquisitiveness can often be just as valuable as those believed to be trusted allies. Remember, friends and foes have different memes of intent.

I was ready to walk into a journey of purposefulness, hoping to render comprehension of an affliction that was continuing to cripple the minds of vulnerable spirits. Some of these afflicted people were not only my peer sufferers but also peer veterans who served their country honorably. I believe that some people fear inaccessibility of advocacies, so the feelings of shame remain, leading many to believe there is no way in and no way out to mental health healing. Mounting questions relating expressive mental behaviors to oppressive mental health are becoming more alarming than ever. The health of an individual's mind is not inescapably dependent upon a person's behavior; on the contrary, recent incidents regarding the infliction of transgressions against others makes for curiosity. I believe that disease intrusion can denigrate the ability to think, which influences incalculably actions, triggering a lapse in judgment. Consequently, a healthy mind usually displays healthy behaviors if and only if adequate care is entered cerebrally to dispel demonic intruders.

Once the mind is ravaged with flooding streams of emotional turmoil, it must be rescued from a power far greater than man. This power is literally breathtaking, allowing a greater power to internally subsist within one's spirit and soul where embodied reservoirs of thought constantly spill over. I assure you, it is not an easy task to fully relinquish yourself and submit perhaps to a power you never conceived of or became acquainted with. I am not suggesting that a spiritual journey for everyone is the same, nor is it the remedy to cure everyone, but for me it was the ultimate therapy to recover.

Some people suffering from mental illness may already have a strong spiritual connection; however, strengthening that connection may lead to different discoveries to cope or amend treatment therapies. My belief is that whenever humankind undergoes life's difficulties, we usually realize there is something more powerfully adroit than us that stabilizes our living. Surrendering to religious destiny may not be true for 100 percent of humanity, but it is credible that at least 80 percent believe in a higher power. The other 20 percent are perhaps of divergent religious beliefs. I had to submit, allowing my vulnerabilities to flow freely as each waterfall revealed an openness to be reflective.

Are you afraid to expose such intimate emotional and mental warfare with those external to your circle, meaning extended worlds of people? Do you believe that only a spiritual deliverance is the cure to mental health survival? Why do you believe you were chosen as an ambassador to rally awareness of mental health illness? These are among the multitude of questions asked by many people, not all in a verbal context. Ironically, some of the questions were asked with a silence of perplexity that sometimes created an invisible barrier. The eavesdroppers appeared tongue-tied as I shared the struggles of mental illness so nakedly.

I refused to swathe any part of my emotional physique with trendy fashions but instead revealed a green style of craze seen with old-fashioned patterns of reality. Momentarily, try not to mistake *craze* for *crazy*, because this is really where thinking may collide with confusion. To rid you of that confusion, it is essential that the three questions above start a dialogue toward godly deliverance. Nevertheless, before I can answer the three interrogations, there was a process to my deliverance.

I returned home one morning after dropping the kids off at school. My husband had left for work, and feeling nothing but isolation, I walked to a room searching for privacy even though I was home alone. I needed to talk to God, not question him, about where I was traveling. My journey was much too confusing and complex for me to understand my direction. So I began to pray to him, praise his name, and worship with a prayer unlike any religious zeal in my past. A season of resurgence was transforming into a harvest to reap, signifying a prevailing test was about to become a compelling testimony.

At first, I kneeled on the floor and began to call out to him so we could connect on holy ground. "Oh my God, I need you," I prayed. "I need answers to questions that I don't even know. God, what is it or what have I done so sinful as to be disconnected from who I am—in such a way of rage, depression, anxiety, fear, phobia, and PTSD, by such demonic powers over my life. Lord, I feel suffocated and gasping for air every day of my life. I awake confused, I feel confused throughout the day, and I go to bed confused. I weep because I'm lonely, unemployed, ill, life's triumphs, family issues, retirement disappointment, and so on. The sad thing is that only you, God, know, and only my family can stand as witnesses to my afflictions.

"Lord," I continued, "I have wanted and tried to end this pain, but you kept me earthly, so there must be a purpose. Crying and sobbing for understanding, I beg you, God, have mercy on my life. Please release and free me from these demons from within my mind, body, and soul. Lord, I cannot defeat Satan without your will. Lord, Satan cannot have me. You said you would never abandon me. So I need you like never before, and I need you to rescue me now, because I cannot take another day living like this.

"Lord," I prayed on, "a change has to come. Lord, I am praying, waddling from knee to belly. I will serve you, oh Lord, and pray daily for my deliverance. God help, help, help me, oh Lord! This is my dying hour, for death is upon my mind, and it seems I am going and coming at the same time. How could this be?"

I prayed to God for days, weeks, and months—a prayer of mercy each day throughout the day and prior to bedtime. I began to strengthen my spiritual growth by frequently reading my Bible, viewing Christian television broadcasts, listening to gospel music, and attending church more frequently. Soon thereafter, I began to sense a rebirth, shifting me from spiritual infancy to spiritual maturity, which was becoming more evident each day. That mystical saying "one day at a time" was clearly all I was asking for. Once again, I felt confident and alive by clear confirmation echoed by a melodious power of speech from thin air that seemingly was a voice from the heavens above.

"My child, it was not about your lack of mental stability; it was all about your lack of spiritual instability. I have a purpose for your life much different from what you imagined! I had to allow you to go through your five-year mental illness affliction to prepare

you for the journey ahead. I needed an ambassador who I could trust to publicly express the mental atrocities inflicted upon my children suffering with mental illness. I am a just God, and their deliverance—just like your deliverance—is within my divine touch. I chose you so that your test can be a testimony of my powerfulness, not mankind's powerlessness. I blessed and favored you with unnatural blessings to assure you that I have all the power, so look at your life and know that there are no more questions, only answers. You have been chosen!"

I was settling into my own skin once again, freed from the ravaging strongholds of mental Illness. A threefold revelation surrounding my purpose was no longer unknown. My new life's purpose was to author, advocate, and be an ambassador to expand public awareness as a surviving veteran resource on mental illness. I like many of my supporters and outsiders had questions that I found difficult or intimidating to respond to. It was not because I was unable to articulate a response, but rather whether I could articulate an acceptable one without feeling ridiculed by shaming. I contemplated whether some of the questions were out of genuine concern or fake countenance from nosey ears with noisy opinions. Frankly, the noise and nosiness were mute in comparison to sharing my spiritual journey.

My journey of recovery must be shared no matter varying perspectives as to the causes of mental illness. Initially, there were many concerns expressed as to whether I was scared to share such intimate details about my journey. My thought was that my illness had been so privatized that it had to be publicized to aid in my recovery. For me, true healing began once I was able to share my feelings and emotions in public forums amongst strangers as well those within my support circle.

My spouse wanted to know how I would react if ridiculed or judged by people who might refer to me as crazy. So, let me be candid as possible. I realize that there are thousands of mentally ill sufferers who were born diseased from a myriad of health issues that impact cerebral functionality; however, this is purely about the infliction of mental illness that may have been inadvertently imposed by an affliction of cause and effect. Therefore, I am not shamed by something that I am grateful and proud to be ridded from the depths of my psychological sensing. Why should I succumb to pressures from those I am unacquainted with and who judge what they themselves are unfamiliar with? Unless you have struggled with the pitfalls of mental illness or are a professional health-care provider, I reject your opinion.

Thus, those who judge are exempted, deemed unfit to render any verdict based solely upon cynical preconceptions regarding guilt of my illness instead of the innocence of my mental healing. Applaud me, clap your hands, hug me, smile at me, and wish me well. God's grace and mercy have revived me. Certainly, I desire a circumference of joy; thus I will not allow insensitive uncertainties to enter my soul of solace. I fought far too long to surrender to the judgment of those who shunned darkened souls like mine, keeping many sufferers from a quality of life where they can live instead of just survive.

Next, a stranger of some sort inquired, is it believable that a person's mental healing must come through the mercies of God? The woman, who seemed of much wisdom, begin to delve into this mystical connection as a regular churchgoer who worked at a Christian school. I suppose she was saved in Jesus's name and filled with the holy ghost. I am not nor would I ever question anyone's religious beliefs, but it was apparent that disbelief was seen in her eyes.

She was stunned that I suffered from mental illness, perhaps like many others, since it was so well hidden. Few if any suspect or inquire because of a perception that mental illness doesn't look like me. She and I had become well acquainted over eighteen months of interaction. No matter how frequently I was in her presence, which was almost daily either by passing or speaking, the lady had no suspicion. As previously mentioned, I am not one to display emotions outwardly unless I sense blatant disregard. Nevertheless, to be in my presence often may evoke at least a pin-hint dropped at some point, unless people are too poker-faced to notice when something is clearly out of place or unusual.

As I think about my ability to evade people's detection of my illness, I believe it was because of God's sheltering grace. His grace kept me safeguarded as he entranced my spirit as a believer to mitigate worldly and gratuitous ridicule. She was probably one of first people I felt comfortable enough with to reveal my illness without feeling angst and stress about being judged. Oddly, her ears and eyes were alerted as I shared intimate accounts about my mental illness clashing with demonic spirits.

My acquaintance was amazed by my triumph over hardships and believed that people diagnosed with mental illness were doomed and could not possibly recover. It was disappointing but also invigorating to my renewed spirituality. I was a walking miracle in the eyes of many. My mental illness deliverance was neither expected nor believable by doubters, yet it was inspiring with rousing devoutness. I recall Bishop T. D. Jakes preaching about those unnatural blessings of favor that only God can step in to deliver.

The lady began sharing people who she knew suffered from mental illness, and I saw her hopelessness turn into hopefulness because of my testimony. After our personal conversation, the lady shared an increasing number of adolescents suffering from mental illness, especially some she knew personally from her spiritual circle. I advised the lady that not all people are the same nor is all deliverances the same. To be frank, some people are birthed with a mental illness, whereas others, like me, experience some level of trauma that inadvertently induces a psychological invasion of emotional warfare—whether from some affliction, injury, or traumatic incident. God had a spoken purpose for my healing, so favor is not always fair …

My initial query of God was clarification of my affliction in the discovery of his purpose for my life. I learned long ago not to question God's intentions; however, I still wanted to know why I was chosen to suffer from such a painful infirmity as mental illness. It was clear once I began to pray for healing that God used me in the flesh to be an ambassador of both this disease and his power. I recognize that spiritual growth is not only a process but also prepares one for the rocky roads ahead. It would be unjust to give me a mission that I could not relate to, aiming to enlighten people of a cause without any experience. It was if my résumé of mental illness ambassadorship had to be through a firsthand encounter.

I now beam about my testimonials because like a job, occupation, or career, there is an expectation of desired qualifications; however, this is not job experience that anyone desires or chooses. Nevertheless, when God deems you qualified, all else is irrelevant. A hospital would not hire a physician without any training or license. If they did, what would be the cost of their liabilities? Therefore, I decided to never ask God, why me? Certainly, I believe God's comeback would have been, "Why not you?" What makes me so different is that I get to choose my triumphs and disappointments in life. I believe God chooses what is both mankind's weakness and strength, producing a harvest that is just, depending upon the season of planting. This allowed me to reap at a time when God yielded favor. I was blessed to recover by divine work invested in my crop of new life.

My belief was that God had chosen me for this saintly endeavor because he cherry-picked someone who did not represent the typical image of someone suffering from mental illness. The mere fact that people were unable to detect the mental health instabilities buried underneath my traumatized skin was perhaps inconceivable. I may never comprehend whether it was an illness conceived at birth, trauma of brain injury, or life's hustle and bustle. I now accept my purposefulness, and each step taken is with the Almighty.

I am reassured by grace with the prayer "Footprints," which corroborates that each of us will need carrying at some point as we travel triumphant journeys. Although this was a journey that I started feeling forlorn and unsure of where I was mysteriously going, I no longer have a loss of sight regarding these mysterious travels that I had to spiritually undergo. I can now see where I am predestined to go. Discover your purposefulness! I had to kneel and then look up, asking God to restore my sanity.

Chapter 17

Imparting Purposefulness: My Beginning to My End

Everyone and everything should have a context of purposefulness. My purpose is to share enlightenment through a lens where a medical affliction is exposed, gaining eye-witnesses. These witnesses must not be muted and reduced to voiceless cries, sobbing for the right to be heard without prosecutorial conviction of inadvertent afflictions. For there is no criminal intent but perhaps felonious guilt by a country that encages psychological and emotional suffering so illness remains hidden and tamed by darkness.

For years, I was afraid to express intimate details of my illness because of deeply embedded reluctance to be publicly vulnerable. I feared criticism for a crime that I did not commit, yet I was condemned and held captive by an infirmity far beyond any keyless entrance or exit. The time has arisen to unmask my suffering secrecy and rise from illness to wellness. This unchained journey to recover from mental illness has been more than defying; at times, mental illness has even been defeated. My purpose is to permit outsiders an insider view, revealing clarity through a voluntarily accessible lens to envision accounts where unruly havoc is inflicted upon the minds of innocents. Insightfulness is the purest form of awareness in the context of comprehending mental illness. We can minimize mental illness strongholds by destroying the very walls that permit undetected entry by acknowledging this communal plea. The plea is to blueprint specific advocacies that promote mental consciousness, offering accessible resources to expand different therapies and aid in illness recovery.

As a sufferer, I often felt barricaded and protected by my layered skin, which was invaded by multiple illnesses, emotions, and fears. These destructive trolls ravaged my mental capacity, peeling away one layer at a time. Frankly, it's incredibly hard work and a feat too mountainous to climb alone, but with communal aid and LAST (love, acknowledgment, support, and time), the feat becomes comprehensibly possible.

When people feel encaged—whether secluded in a room or in the world—eventually they will become a detriment to not only themselves but those surrounding them. The inner walls that once seemingly protected me like many other mental illness sufferers started to seep frightful light. The light exposing deeply held secrets from my external world created a glare that was both unusual and unpredictable. I believed that if I revealed too much or too soon without contemplating the backlash, it would possible exacerbate my fear of being exposed.

The four walls that often cornered my emotions must now unlock entries and exits to permit those suffering to breathe with solace. Renewal must take place within the depths of three elements: the spirit, soul, and mind. Contrary to these three essentials, the most critical start is perhaps having you and I as ambassadors. A platform of advocacy is vital to motivate therapeutic relationships that spark heartfelt change. Mental illness sufferers must not continue to be or feel like suffering hostages, so release these chains. I am all in. Are you?

I encourage everyone to get to know your true GEMS—that is, faith, family, and friends. Faith is humanely greater than all things. Family is genetically everything, and true friends are customarily more supportive than most, especially those who offer unconditional love. These comforting entities are of relational significance. They are imparted upon each of us to celebrate each milestone while also conveying relentless advocacy during times of adversity.

My circle of GEMS is private and personal but certainly not squared by barricades of exclusion; thus, we inclusively share our dreams and fears as we brandish real emotions. A true gem reflects a spirit of solidarity even if the spotlight sparkles brighter on one side more than the other. In the end, we all shine bright like diamonds, even when the light appears somewhat dimmed,

Sacred GEMS: Homages

Mrs. Lula La'Belle Landown
Mom

I would like to thank my mom for birthing a warrior! I grew up determined to be a resilient trailblazer, following steps of measured relevance and the service of my deceased veteran father. You instilled ethical values that taught me how to be a winner even if I had to lose, revealing the true essence of humility. Thanks for being in my corner—for even my insulated walls revealed secret cracks over time. I am now refurbished with new beginnings and a different window of sight. Mother, your cemented bond of connectivity continues to strengthen our mother–daughter relationship from my birth to even now. Our bond of unity is inseparable!

Sandra C. Landown
Sisterly Solace

You are an inspiration to continue this journey of life, motivating our family to travel its destination to stillness. Your spirit, laughter, and love of life were the epitome of pure calmness that you relentlessly demonstrated throughout your malaises that masked your spirit far too soon. We are proud of you and the three gifts of life extant for us to relish as we move onward. You are and will always be our spirited sunshine, whether sunrise or sunset. Life is transitorily all so changeable.

Mrs. Traci Nelson-Williams
Career Mentor

Mentors are like conductors of a moving train. They discern when to speed up and when to slow down, allowing the commuter to observe and engage simultaneously. You never commanded unattainable expectations that would wreck my speed of progression, stagnating movement toward an all-aboard career destination. I so much benefited from the times when you were the engine and even the caboose. Your interchangeability as my leader permitted my talents to intersect; whether I sat upfront, in the middle, or at the rear. Thanks for the exploration throughout my career; without you refining my engine, I may have exhausted my value long ago, not comprehending my lifelong worth.

Ms. Marcelle Burroni
Benevolent Fairy Forevermore (BFF)

A best friend is not only a confidant but also a believer during a friend's most vulnerable and uncertain time, cheering for her during her struggles, encouraging her during her failures, cautioning her when she gets off track, but most poignantly loving her when she is absent in spirit. You have been all that and too much to mention. Thus, your imprint in my heart is forevermore etched and can never be uprooted. Our incomparable sisterhood is deeper than the sea and higher than mountains, for you have coupled me far beyond the depths of the earth and the highs of the blue skies. Thanks for embracing me through times of struggle, for I know my confidences are buried in the gravities of our souls.

Princess Landowyn A. Clarke
Angelic Daughter

You are a true princess, and your presence in my life is magically enthroned by the purity of your existence. You came into my life with a purpose that is yet perplexing but also so incredible. I prayed eight years for you and had spiritually surrendered my faith, doubting that God would answer my prayer. You rebirthed my faith, my life, and my will to live again. Coincidentally, when I thought I was answering your pampered cries, it was instead God's mercy triggering your fateful cry to rescue my life from an impulsive demise. I am forever grateful for your love and your spirited light; thus, you lighten spaces of dimness with flameless luminosity, offering a smile that is oh so bright.

Gina Szafner known as GiGiS
Book Designer

Thank you for canvassing my psychological and emotional mysteries!

About the Author

The author is a proud mom of three as well an adept wife and warrior who confronts mental illness face-to-face. During her five-year-long psychological encounter, she became captive to a powerful, demonic spirit that constantly battered her emotions. This mental imprisonment impeded her will to exit as well became an opposition for anyone to enter to offer a lifeline for survival. It was determined by medical diagnosis that her military service as a combat veteran contributed to her immeasurable successes over her twenty-two-year career but was also a major contributor to the demise of her mental and emotional health.

Oftentimes, people like the author become subjected to inaccurate sentiments without insight regarding mental illness, all based upon unsubstantiated yet descriptive perceptions surrounding the disorder. The author is an accomplished military officer; an MBA graduate; and now an author. The phrase, "You don't look sick" is the connotation that centralizes the theme of the book's title, "MI Doesn't Look Like ME." No one can say for certain what mental illness looks like, but the author reveals it felt like during some of her darkest days. She depicts mental illness as a relentless, raging storm that never rests. The author recalls that the illness at times seemed to accompany foes with a premeditated intent to destroy her mind, body, and soul. She fought this life-suffocating sentence induced by mental illness while struggling to free her mind. After her mind was freed, her body became unshackled, unleashing fragmented chains and empowering her to write and share this story!

2017 NATIONAL MENTAL HEALTH OBSERVANCES

Month	National Mental Health Observances	Suggested Themes
January	National Drug Facts Week (Jan.23-29); Fun at Work Day (Jan. 27)	A Healthy New Year
February	American Heart Month; National School Counseling Week (Feb. 6-10); Random Acts of Kindness Week (Feb.12-18); National Eating Disorders Awareness Week (Feb. 26- Mar.4)	Eating Disorders and Mental Health
March	American National Nutrition Month; Employee Spirit Month; Developmental Disabilities Awareness Month; National Sleep Awareness Week (Mar. 2-9); Brain Awareness Week (Mar. 13-19); World Bipolar Day (Mar. 30)	Nutrition and Mental Health
April	National Autism Awareness Month; Alcohol Awareness Month; National Minority Mental Health Month; National Counseling Awareness Month; National Stress Awareness Month; National Workplace Wellness Week (TBD); World Health Day (Apr. 7)	Workplace Wellness

2017 NATIONAL MENTAL HEALTH OBSERVANCES

Month	National Mental Health Observances	Suggested Themes
May	**Mental Health Month; Children's Mental Health Awareness Week (13-17); National Prevention Week (May 14-20); Older Americans' Mental Health Week (TBD); Schizophrenia Awareness Week (TBD); National Mental Health and Dignity Day (TBD); National Anxiety and Depression Awareness Week (May 7-13); Children's Mental Health Awareness Day (May 4)**	Mental Health Awareness
June	PTSD Awareness Month; National Post-traumatic Stress Disorder Awareness Day (June 27)	Trauma and PTSD
July	**National Minority Mental Health Awareness Month**	Cultural Competency
August	No official national mental health observances scheduled.	Back-to-School Preventative Care

2017 NATIONAL MENTAL HEALTH OBSERVANCES

Month	National Mental Health Observances	Suggested Themes
September	**National Recovery Month; National Alcohol & Drug Addiction Recovery Month; National Suicide Prevention Week (Sept. 10-16); World Suicide Prevention Day (Sept. 10)**	Suicide Prevention Recovery Month
October	**National Depression and Mental Health Screening Month; Health Literacy Month; ADHD Awareness Month; Bullying Prevention Month; Mental Illness Awareness Week (Oct.1-7); National Depression Screening Day (Oct.5); World Mental Health Day (Oct.10); OCD Awareness Week (TBD); National Bipolar Awareness Day (TBD)**	World Mental Health
November	**International Survivors of Suicide Day (Nov.18)**	Suicide Survivors
December	**National Stress-Free Family Holiday's Month; International Day of Persons With Disabilities (Dec.3)**	Stress-less This Season

Printed in the United States
By Bookmasters